WITHDRAWN

A PLUME BOOK

HOW TO DATE MEN

JANIS SPINDEL is the author of the bestselling dating guide *Get Serious About Getting Married: 365 Proven Ways to Find Love in Less Than a Year* (HarperCollins/Regan Books, 2005). She is the founder and president of Janis Spindel Serious Matchmaking, Inc., and has over 760 marriages and 1,100 long-term, committed relationships to her credit. She is a former fashion executive and has been featured in hundreds of magazine and newspaper articles. She lives in New York City with her husband of twenty-four years (her first successful match!) and her two daughters.

Janis Spindel

How to Date Men

*Dating Secrets from
America's Top Matchmaker*

A PLUME BOOK

PLUME

Published by Penguin Group

Penguin Group (USA) Inc., 375 Hudson Street, New York, New York 10014, U.S.A. •
Penguin Group (Canada), 90 Eglinton Avenue East, Suite 700, Toronto, Ontario, Canada
M4P 2Y3 (a division of Pearson Penguin Canada Inc.) • Penguin Books Ltd., 80 Strand,
London WC2R 0RL, England • Penguin Ireland, 25 St. Stephen's Green, Dublin 2, Ireland
(a division of Penguin Books Ltd.) • Penguin Group (Australia), 250 Camberwell Road,
Camberwell, Victoria 3124, Australia (a division of Pearson Australia Group Pty. Ltd.) •
Penguin Books India Pvt. Ltd., 11 Community Centre, Panchsheel Park, New Delhi – 110
017, India • Penguin Group (NZ), 67 Apollo Drive, Rosedale, North Shore 0745, Auckland,
New Zealand (a division of Pearson New Zealand Ltd.) • Penguin Books (South Africa)
(Pty.) Ltd., 24 Sturdee Avenue, Rosebank, Johannesburg 2196, South Africa

Penguin Books Ltd., Registered Offices: 80 Strand, London WC2R 0RL, England

First published by Plume, a member of Penguin Group (USA) Inc.

First Printing, September 2007

10 9 8 7 6 5 4 3 2 1

AUTHOR'S NOTE: The individual experiences recounted in this book are true. However,
names and descriptive details have been changed to protect the identities of the persons
involved.

℗ REGISTERED TRADEMARK—MARCA REGISTRADA

LIBRARY OF CONGRESS CATALOGING-IN-PUBLICATION DATA
Spindel, Janis, 1951–
  How to date men : dating secrets from America's top matchmaker / Janis Spindel.
    p. cm.
ISBN 978-0-452-28867-6 (trade pbk.)
1. Dating (Social customs) 2. Man-woman relationships. I. Title.

HQ801.S687 2007

646.7'7082—dc22

                                                                2007006158

Printed in the United States of America
Set in Esprit Book

For Allen, Carly, and Falyn

Acknowledgments

I always need to start by thanking my father, Norman Siderman, because without him nothing I've done or accomplished in life would have been possible (literally!). He continues to amaze me every day, and he's still going strong at eighty-nine! I'm pretty much his personality clone. Whenever people ask me about influences in my life, I just say, "You need to meet my father!" Thanks also to my darling mother, Luba, and my loving siblings, Warren, Ilene, and Marsha.

This book would not have been possible without the effort and guidance of my fabulous agent, Jennifer Joel. Simply put, she's the absolute best! I also want to thank her assistant, Katie Sigelman, as well as everyone else at ICM who helped out.

The entire staff at Plume has been great to work with, most especially my editor, Emily Haynes, who's been enthusiastic about this book every step of the way. Both Emily and Jennifer are the sort of dynamic, intelligent women that I'm lucky enough to come across in my work.

But, of course, this was a book about men, so I needed a guy in the mix as well. A very special thanks to Peter Scott, who did an incredible job of putting all my ideas and advice into words. Peter, if you weren't already married, I'd set you up!

I know that I drive my lawyer, Roz Lichter, totally crazy by calling her a thousand times a day with a million questions and concerns. But, thankfully, she's very patient and wise. I'm beyond lucky to have her on my team.

While I was working on the book, my wonderful assistants made sure Janis Spindel Serious Matchmaking, Inc., was always running smoothly. Girls, I'd be lost without you!

And finally, I want to thank my husband, Allen Spindel, and my daughters, Carly and Falyn. The three of you are the best family a matchmaker could ever have.

Contents

Introduction

Ladies, I've got news for you—if you're still single and frustrated about it, it means one of two things:

1. You're super picky

   OR

2. You're doing something wrong

Let me guess: You tell people that you're super picky, right? But you know as well as I do that you're probably doing something wrong.

Well, it's time to start doing things the right way. And for those of you who are still in denial, remember this: If you truly are the pickiest person in the world (which I *seriously* doubt), then that's all the more reason to make sure you're doing everything the right way. I mean, you don't want to blow your one-in-a-million chance when the right guy finally does come along!

You've obviously realized by now that the hardest part about dating is trying to figure out what's going on inside a man's head—most of time, women are beyond clueless.

Women almost always express their thoughts and emotions

better than men. Which means that guys generally have a good sense of what women are after—someone who's smart, loyal, and has a great sense of humor.

If men talked about their feelings as much as women do, then dating would be easy. But we all know there's not a chance in China that's going to happen. So how do you find out what men really want if they don't tell you?

You can ask your girlfriends what he really meant when he said he had "a nice time" with you and whether the third date is too soon to have sex. But your girlfriends will say what they think you want to hear because they don't want to hurt your feelings. And besides, when they answer your questions, they're guessing. They don't have the real answers.

But I do. And they're all in this book.

Now, I know what you're thinking:

Um, Janis, why should I trust you?! You're not a guy!

You're right! I'm not a guy. But I *am* a professional match-maker. In 1993 I formed my own company, Janis Spindel Serious Matchmaking, Inc., to help bring ambitious, time-starved singles together. I knew I had the uncanny knack for adjusting Cupid's arrow because prior to going professional, *fourteen* different couples I introduced in one year ALL ended up getting married!

What separates me from other matchmakers out there is that I have clairvoyant premonitions about people. I know that sounds really weird, but there's no other way to explain it. I just have a sixth sense about matchmaking. I help facilitate love. I turn first dates into second dates, second dates into third dates, and third dates into marriage proposals.

Most importantly, *all of my clients are men*. My entire business is about understanding what men want in a relationship. That's how I make my living. One of the first things a new client and I will do is go on a simulated date. On that date I'll give him the "I Dream of Jeannie" test. I tell him to pretend that I can magically twitch my nose and make the woman of his dreams appear. All he has to do is describe her to me.

Obviously, not all men are the same. But I hear an awful lot of the same things over and over again. And I'll tell you one thing: *Men are picky*! When one of my set-ups doesn't work out, 90 percent of the time it's because the guy isn't interested in or attracted to the woman. Sorry, ladies, that's the reality.

Luckily for you, though, I've helped to create over 760 marriages in my thirteen years of professional matchmaking, so, all modesty aside, I'm confident that I know what I'm talking about.

Besides my own expertise, this book is loaded with quotes from my clients. That's right: You're getting real advice from real men. You'll read about their thoughts on everything, from how to get their phone number to when they want to meet your parents . . . and all the steps in between.

The Big Picture

Now that you know my credentials, let's talk about you. The goal of this book is *not* to change you into someone else so that you can meet more men. Believe me . . . guys *don't* want that! In fact, the number-one complaint I hear from my clients is that they hate women who seem to be one thing during the first few dates and then suddenly change into someone else later in the relationship.

> *"Do not act inconsistently. Stability is something that gets high scores among men. If we sense you acting differently from our first date, then we get red flags."*
>
> —Adam, New York, NY

What I want to do with this book is *educate* you about what men are looking for so your own dating life will be more successful. I'm going to do this in two ways:

1. I'm going to give you the answers to all those questions you have about what guys are thinking, such as, "If he paid for the first date, should I pay for the second one?" or "Do I need to watch the NFL playoffs with him?" or "Is he expecting sex on his birthday . . . and if so, how much?"

2. I'm going to point out all the ways in which you've probably been doing things wrong up to this point in your dating life. You may think you know what makes men tick, but you don't . . . at least, not yet.

The good news is that the one thing all men are definitely looking for is something that you can have: confidence. Confidence is the true aphrodisiac for men—it *really* turns them on. If you're happy with who you are, then he will be too. I always tell people that I can bring a horse to water, but I can't make him drink. At the end of the day, I can set people up, but the falling in love is up to you.

Even the greatest guy will notice whatever aspects of yourself you don't like. If you hate your body, he will too. If this sounds really harsh, remember that you should hold men to the same standard. If he doesn't feel like he's very successful, why would you disagree?

Remember that a boyfriend will not magically cure everything that's wrong in your life. You already have to like your life before you have a boyfriend. A good guy will want to help make things even better, but only if it's clear that he'll be sharing the heavy lifting with you.

> *"I don't like it when a woman tells me what she needs from a guy. My personal view is that we should each seek out what the other person needs, not tell them [directly]. Making someone else happy makes a good relationship. Demanding what you want does not."*
>
> —Henry, New York, NY

Book Structure

This book is organized into four sections:

Part 1: The Beginning

What are men looking for in the very beginning of a relationship? This section will examine the how and the where of meeting each other, the exchanging of phone numbers, the preparations for the first date, and then, most importantly, the actual first date.

I'll also discuss the topic that keeps most single women up at night: their body. The reality: Looks matter, and they matter a lot. The good news: I'm here to help!

Part 2: I Think We're Dating

What causes a guy to stop referring to you as "this girl I went out with," and start referring to you as "my girlfriend"? I'll discuss the second and third dates, the first night together, and the always important meeting of each other's friends.

Part 3: The Happy Couple

What does a guy want in a serious, long-term relationship? In this section we'll analyze what men are looking for during romantic weekend trips away, special occasions such as birthdays and Valentine's Day, and the most nerve-wracking event of them all: the meeting of each other's families.

Part 4: The One

In this final section, I'll reveal what a guy is looking for in his lifelong partner. What makes a man realize he's in a relationship that he wants to stay in forever? When's the right time to talk about the subject of marriage? And how do you subtly tell him not to buy a pear-shaped diamond?

Not What You're After

A woman who wants a serious relationship (YOU!) needs to be cautious of a man who says that he's interested in the same thing, when, in fact, his idea of a "serious relationship" equals only "knows your last name." A single man is like a little boy in a candy store: Sometimes he's having too much fun to commit to just one piece.

When this book discusses what men are looking for, I'm referring to those men who are also in the market for a serious relationship (don't worry—there are millions of them!). But at the end of each chapter, I'll provide a "Not What You're After" section to help you recognize the danger signs that suggest you may be with a man who claims to want something serious, when in reality he's only slightly more evolved than a bowl of chocolate pudding (and far less delicious).

Let Him Down Easy

This section will instruct you on how to break up with a guy if you realize he isn't the one for you. Like it or not ladies, you are also capable of being sharks. If you don't like a guy, you need to throw him back into the sea in one piece so that another woman has the chance to catch him. Don't chew him up emotionally and spit him out in little bits because that's (a) gross and (b) unfair to all the other single girls out there (not to mention the guy!). Remember: Men gossip too. If you get a reputation as a man-eater, dates will suddenly become much harder to get.

So let's get started. You're about to discover that dating men is so much easier when you have all the answers right in front of you.

Part One

The Beginning

CHAPTER 1

The Origins of the Boyfriend
Before Your Paths Ever Cross

Let's start off this chapter with a little quiz:

Which of the following statements is true?

1. The man of your dreams is out there somewhere.
2. You'll know him when you see him.

Okay, let me guess: You said the second statement is true. You're not sure if the man of your dreams really exists, but if he does, you'll know him when you see him.

Well, I've got some news for you—you're wrong. From my experience as a matchmaker, I know that the first statement is totally true: Your perfect guy is out there in the world somewhere (and I'm going to help you find him!).

Actually, if I'm being completely honest, ladies, there's really *more than one* perfect guy for you. If there was only one person for everyone, then no one you know would be married because they'd only have a one in six billion chance of finding their spouse! Luckily, it's a lot easier than that.

However, there's a good chance that your Prince Charming is different from the image you have of him from your childhood fantasies. I don't mean to suggest that he won't be a fabulous guy—he will be! But his job, appearance, and favorite TV show may be different from how you picture it.

Why? Because men, like women, don't grow up in plastic toy boxes. If you want to date a Ken doll, go down to Toys "Я" Us and knock yourself out. But back here in reality, the man of your dreams has been busy being shaped by his family, his education, his friends, and, most importantly, his past relationships.

A lot of women think they can try to change guys to fit a preexisting image they have in their mind. That NEVER works because by the time someone makes it to their late twenties and thirties, they're already going to have an identity. So you need to figure out if his identity works with yours. Before you meet your Fantasy Man face to face, I think it's best if you get to know him a little bit better.

> *"Don't try to change me into someone else. I'll just revert back to being me in the long run, anyway."*
>
> —Charlie, New York, NY

From Several Billion to a Couple Hundred

Let's start with *who* men are looking for. Imagine that you are a single guy. It seems pretty great, right? You don't have to worry about giving birth, paying a fortune for haircuts, or having people raise an eyebrow when you order dessert. On the flip side, you do have to shave your face every day, and if you miss a spot everyone will notice and think you're a moron.

I digress. As a single guy, you're going to want to narrow down the three billion women in the world into a (much) smaller group that contains women you would actually be interested in dating.

Now, most women will be eliminated by obvious factors like marital status, age, and where they live—a thirty-five-year-old guy in Los Angeles probably isn't going to want to date a sixty-year-old housewife from Finland.

But even if we're only talking about single women who live in the same area code as you, there are still going to be lots of ladies you don't want to date. Maybe you're a lawyer and really want someone with the same career so she can understand your crazy work schedule. Maybe you grew up in Canada and love the idea of finding a fellow Canuck. Maybe you have a thing for Buddhists. Trust me . . . I've literally seen it all. Nothing surprises me at this point.

Let's snap out of the pretending-we're-guys fantasy, and realize the point I'm trying to make:

Important Thing to Realize About Single Men

NOT EVERY MAN IS GOING TO BE INTERESTED IN YOU, NO MATTER HOW BEAUTIFUL, SMART, OR SUCCESSFUL YOU ARE.

Each guy will have his own individual criteria, which means that for some men, you'll be eliminated before you even meet.

Now, don't freak out on me and start thinking something like this:

Janis, what if his criteria are unrealistic? What if he wants a Phi Beta Kappa who's six feet tall with blonde hair, C-cup breasts, a high-ranking job at Vogue, *and, of course, weighs under a hundred pounds.*

You're right—there are guys out there who have criteria like that. And some of them are my clients! But guess what? *If a guy has unrealistic expectations, that's his problem, not yours.* Guys who want a woman that doesn't exist (or that they're never going to get) have got some issues to work out. But you're not his therapist, so don't spend time worrying about it. Move on to someone else.

Here's a hilarious story that proves my point: I have a client, Tony, who came to me with a list of *a hundred* things he was looking for in a woman. I'm not kidding! He literally had one hundred characteristics he thought he needed in a girl-friend! And they were all so specific! Comments like: She has to like to go skiing, but not every weekend in January.

Needless to say, there was a big problem. I said, "Tony, I'm not a custom-made service here! You're being ridiculous!" Tony resisted at first, giving all the usual excuses like, "I've done a lot of thinking about this, Janis!" or "I know what I want, I just can't find it." I finally convinced Tony to go out on a date with a woman who met some, but not all one hundred, of his prerequisites (maybe she liked to go skiing in February and not January). And guess what happened? Tony had a great time. Now, he didn't wind up dating that first woman, but he came to realize that he was being ridiculous.

You can think you know what you want, but that usually goes right out the window when a special person comes along. This holds true for men *and* women.

> *"If you say you're looking for a nice guy and you meet one, then give him a chance, even though he may not be your look."*
>
> —Link, San Francisco, CA

Luckily, most guys are open-minded. They may have thought when they were twelve that they were going to date Elle Macpherson, but now, at age thirty, they know that dating a *Sports Illustrated* swimsuit model ain't going to happen. (In fact, they probably knew that ten years ago; they just had to live in denial for a bit.)

Guys generally build a lot of wiggle room into their criteria. Here's what I mean:

Criteria	You Think That Means	In Reality, It Just Means
Someone athletic	Triathlete	Someone with a gym membership
Someone intelligent	Yale	A college he's heard of
Someone worldly	Jet-setter	You don't count a trip to the Venetian in Las Vegas as "having been to Italy"
Someone hip	Shops only at Prada	Shops somewhere else besides Wal-Mart
Someone successful	Oprah	You make enough money to avoid living with your parents

All of this is just a fancy way of saying that while you'll definitely be the wrong match for some guys, you're going to be a real possibility for a lot of them. Men will go into a relationship with an open mind if you do as well.

"Leave your old impressions behind. Start with a clean slate."

—Matt, Los Angeles, CA

Location, Location, Location

So now that you know who single men are after, let's talk about *where* guys are hoping to meet women. The stereotype with men is that they're never too busy to meet a woman they think will sleep with them. That may be true, but most guys are more evolved than that. In reality, men are never too busy to meet an *interesting* woman.

Here's a list of places that probably come to mind when you think about where guys like to meet women:

Obvious Places Where Men Like to Meet Women

- ♥ Weddings
- ♥ The workplace
- ♥ Dinner/cocktail parties
- ♥ College alumni events
- ♥ The home of a mutual friend

This list is good, but it could be better. Why? *Because men feel that anyplace is a good place to meet women.*

In fact, I think it's actually easier to meet people when you're focusing on what you're doing, not who you're with. When you're in a bar, there's too much pressure to be "on" and look "datable." But if you're playing tennis or standing in line at Office Depot, you won't be concentrating on meeting people, which actually makes it easier and more natural to strike up a conversation.

And I'll say it again because it's so important: A guy is just as happy meeting someone great at Office Depot as he is meeting them at a bar. Seriously. If a guy is being wheeled into surgery and he feels a spark with his female doctor, he makes a mental note to ask her out to dinner when he wakes up (unless she messes up the surgery, in which case he may have bigger problems!).

So in addition to the list above, here's a bunch of other places where my clients have told me they've picked up women:

Not-So-Obvious Places Where Men Like to Meet Women

- ♥ Standing in line at the DMV
- ♥ Jury duty
- ♥ Department stores
- ♥ Airplanes
- ♥ Sporting events
- ♥ Museums

Men are always on the lookout, which means that you need to be too! Love often happens when you least expect it. Just because you're standing in line at a Starbucks doesn't mean you can't meet someone. I mean, hello—you already know you have something in common: You both drink coffee! I'm not saying you have to wear a sexy dress twenty-four hours a day. This could be a bit of problem if your occupation is, say, a police officer. But just because it's 7:45 in the morning and you're in your power suit doesn't mean you can't get the phone number of that cute guy who's hitting on you as you both wait for your lattes.

Bottom line: If you're only interested in meeting men between 8 p.m. and 11 p.m. on Friday nights, it's never going to happen, because that's not the only time when men want to meet you.

Ain't Nothing Like the Real Thing

When it comes to *how* men like to meet women, their favorite way is, of course, on their own. There's nothing easier than falling in love with your coworker, your neighbor, your old friends from school, and so on.

While lots of people do find love this way, we all know that leaving it to chance doesn't always work out. If you were in love with your neighbor and he was in love with you, then I'm willing to bet you wouldn't have bought this book in the first place!

Sometimes we're not lucky enough to have the perfect guy fall on our lap. We have to go out and get him. And for my money, there's just no substitute for a personal recommendation. I'm not saying you have to use a professional matchmaker. Instead, men love to use their friends. Here's why:

A friend knows him better than anyone. Who is a guy going to trust more: his closest friend from college or a computer program? There's an X-factor involved with matchmaking that Internet dating can never capture.

You can meet before the date. If a friend wants to set a guy up with someone, he or she can arrange a group meeting in advance of the date. If you're both at a birthday party, for example, you can say hello, chat for a bit, and decide for yourselves if you want to go out.

It's free. I'll be the first to admit that hiring me as a matchmaker is not cheap. I completely understand that not everyone can or wants to spend money on a matchmaker. Luckily, a setup from a friend doesn't cost a dime.

Since guys like to meet women through mutual friends, what does that mean for you? A few things:

1. Let your friends know that you're open to the idea of being set up. Recommending a date is a very personal gesture and even your close friends won't want to do this without permission.

2. If you want something unusual, let them know. You friends are probably going to assume that you want someone who's the same age, race, and religion as you. So if you want to meet someone outside of that group, be sure and let them know, or it won't happen.

3. When your friends invite you places to meet people, go! This is so obvious, and yet many women don't do it. You tell your friends that you want to be set up, but then, when they invite you over to a dinner party on Wednesday night, you say you have a lot of work to catch up on and then you go home. Unacceptable! You need to change your plans and go over to your friend's place. The more you say no, the less effort your friends will make in the future.

> *"If you say dating is a priority, then act like it. Make yourself available. No excuses like 'I have to go to the gym tonight' or 'I'm with my girlfriends this weekend.'"*
> —Link, San Francisco, CA

4. Thank your friends even if the date is a disaster. Sometimes a setup doesn't go well. That's life. But don't take it out on your friends. They were just trying to help. Be polite about it. Remember: They're the ones doing you a favor. And they also may set you up with Mr. Perfect down the line so you don't want to discourage them!

You Can't Ignore Technology

Even though I always recommend meeting people the old-fashioned way, I know some people will disagree:

I know personal recommendations are great, but meeting people on the Internet is just so convenient!

Look, I'm realistic. But you should know that Internet dating is not as simple as first meets the eye. Women always lie about their age and their weight and men always lie about their age and their height. And that's just the tip of the iceberg:

You think: I can screen people to be sure they have the same interests as me. For example, you love food, and would love to meet someone else who is into fine dining.

Reality: The guy may say he's a food lover on his profile, but his interpretation of what that means may differ from yours. You think being a foodie means you try lots of different cuisines from all over the world. He may think it means going to the same restaurant every week and always getting the salmon salad.

You think: I can meet hundreds of guys without ever leaving my desk.

Reality: You aren't really "meeting" them, are you? You're reading about them, which is completely different. That's why most Internet dates begin to feel less like a romantic evening out and more like a job interview.

You think: I can take a personality test that will help match me with people I'm compatible with.

Reality: Ever heard of computer error? And, seriously ladies, do you really want to base your dating pool on a multiple choice test?

You think: Everyone knows that Internet dates don't always work out, so there's less pressure for the date to succeed.

Reality: How depressing is that?! People tend to have such low expectations before a date that the evening becomes a self-fulfilling prophecy— and a waste of time.

You think: I can tell which guys are interested in a serious relationship by reading their profile.

Reality: The sad truth: *a lot* of men online are just looking to hook up, even if they state otherwise. I see it happen all the time. Sorry . . . that's the truth.

If you do decide to try a little Internet dating, there are a few things you can do to help increase the odds of meeting the right guy:

Be honest. Don't lie in your online profile. Guys will quickly find out that you lied and they'll be really annoyed.

Be responsive. If a guy e-mails you and you're interested, don't wait. The longer you think it over, the less excited he'll become.

Research the guy. This is a complaint that I've heard from a couple of men. Don't ignore what he writes on his profile just because you disagree with it. If he says on his profile that he wants a woman who will quit her career when it's time to have kids, you need to be aware of that if you choose to date him!

Be enthusiastic. Everyone knows that Internet dates can be a disaster. But if you're going to do it, embrace it. Don't send him dull, depressing e-mails. If you sound like you'd rather have dinner alone, that's exactly what will happen.

Be realistic. Don't be overly upset if a guy turns out to be not quite what you expected. Even if he was totally honest in his online profile, it's hard to really know if you're a match until you meet face to face.

I think the best thing to do is have a combination of personal recommendations and Internet dates. Your friends aren't going to recommend a new person every day. So if you have some downtime before the next setup, hit that computer. If your Internet dates are a disaster, at least you have the peace of mind of knowing that a personal recommendation is on the way soon.

The Right Time

Finally, let's discuss *when* men want a serious relationship. Women always assume that if a guy is interested in dating, he must also be interested in getting married because that's how they operate. For us girls there tends to be two choices when it comes to dating: something serious or something casual. And you're obviously ready for something serious—that's why you have this book.

But—news flash!—men don't always see things the same way as women do. For a guy, there are about a hundred dating categories, including:

- ♥ We see each other twice a week but only at her place, and I don't keep any stuff there.
- ♥ We're seriously committed to each other . . . until the inevitable breakup in about six months.
- ♥ I'm totally in love with her. Of course, she lives in Europe and we see each other three times a year.
- ♥ I definitely would consider marrying her in about six years.
- ♥ She comes with me to work events and other things when I need a date, but we intentionally don't talk about personal stuff like dating and relationships. Oh, and we have sex ten times a week.

If I told an eighteen-year-old girl that she'll meet her husband when she's twenty-two, she'll probably be thrilled. But if I tell an eighteen-year-old guy that same news, he'll freak out. Why? Because a man feels the need to sow his wild oats more than a woman does. It takes men a while to warm up to the idea that they'll only be having sex with one person for the rest of their life (even if they're currently having sex with *nobody*!).

Yes, some guys go through this phase of their life much quicker than others. On average, though, remember this:

> A GUY PROBABLY ISN'T THINKING SERIOUSLY ABOUT MARRIAGE UNTIL AT LEAST HIS LATE TWENTIES.

So for you, the single woman, try to remember that:

1. It's okay to try to get a serious commitment from a twenty-four-year-old, but you're going to have a lot more success with a thirty-four-year-old.

2. Guy in his early twenties + talk about marriage = 99 percent chance of him freaking out.

3. If a young guy doesn't want to commit to you, don't take it personally. Just decide whether you want to wait . . . and if you don't, then move on.

Now, a quick word on the other side of the occasion, namely: *your* age. Women are always telling me the following:

Janis, here's the problem. When a guy turns thirty and is ready to settle down, isn't he going to want to marry some young girl who's twenty-three? If I'm thirty-four, am I destined to date men who are ten to fifteen years older than me?

Look, there's no denying that there are marriages out there involving an older man and a (much) younger girl. *But those marriages are the exception, not the rule.* It may seem like those marriages are the norm because they tend to generate the most amount of gossip. But the reality is that when a man wants to seriously start dating, he's going to turn to his peer group first. So if you're thirty-four, you can totally find a husband who's in his thirties and not his fifties.

Not What You're After

Ladies, be careful about guys who haven't done a lot of thinking about *who* they want to date. I know that may sound weird:

He says he's open to meeting anyone. Isn't that a good thing?

In theory, yes, it's a good thing. In reality, it usually means he's not ready for a serious relationship.

If a guy is really interested in settling down, he's going to spend some time thinking about whether he wants a Democrat versus a Republican, a lawyer versus an artist, or a Beatles fan versus a Stones junkie. Saying that he's given the matter no thought sounds cool on the surface, but usually spells doom.

Let Him Down Easy

I know it's a little early in the book to tell you about how to break up with a guy and "let him down easy"—I mean, you're not even dating him yet! But there's a really important point I need to make:

> WHEN A MAN TELLS YOU HE ISN'T
> READY TO SETTLE DOWN, LISTEN TO HIM!

Or, to put it another way, don't ignore it when a man tells you that he's still in the wild and crazy part of his "when" phase. A lot of women think that they can make a guy mature faster by dating or sleeping with him. Well, I've got news for you: *It's not going to happen.*

Think about it. Why would he change? He already gets to sleep with you! He's going to act exactly as he told you he would, and you'll be upset that he doesn't want to get more serious. You'll eventually have a fight and things will end badly.

So if a guy is considerate enough to tell you the truth, listen to him! Just move on to someone else. And, most importantly, there's no need to make him feel bad about not being ready to settle down. I know TONS of women who do this and it never makes any sense to me. Yelling at a guy isn't going to push him closer to marriage—it's going to scare him away! And then he's going to stop being so honest with his next girlfriend. That's even worse.

CHAPTER 2

Do You Come Here Often?

The First Time You Meet Each Other

One of the things I do as a matchmaker is give speeches to large groups of women about the do's and don'ts of dating. I fly all over the country giving these speeches and I absolutely love doing it. Why? Well, women have so many questions about dating and it makes me really happy to be able to give some answers—real answers from real experiences, not some made up garbage designed to make you feel better (or worse!).

One of the questions I get asked EVERY TIME I give a speech is:

When I meet a guy I like, can I make the first move?

The answer to the question is yes . . . most of the time.

The easiest situation is if we're talking about someone you already know. If the two of you are already acquainted, then we're full steam ahead. *Go for it! Ask him out!* He may say no, but he'll be flattered that you were interested in him and had the courage to do something about it.

If we're talking about someone whom you've literally just met, it gets slightly more complicated. Guys are still thrilled to have you make the first move, but there are some important exceptions:

Situations Where You SHOULDN'T Make the First Move

He's talking to another woman one on one. A lot of women think that interrupting a conversation will flatter a man's ego and make him pay attention to you. No! The only thing he'll be thinking is that you're incredibly rude. He'll remember you, but for all the wrong reasons.

He's in the middle of doing something that requires concentration. Okay, let's say you're at a wedding and you've been flirting all night with the best man. When is the best time to ask for his number? Well, it's not when he's nervously grabbing the microphone to give his toast.

He's in the middle of a serious conversation with a bunch of guys. This is a tricky situation to spot, because men generally don't have complete breakdowns in public. But if you see a guy huddled in the corner of a bar with some friends and he's got an angry look on his face, it's probably not the ideal moment to ask if he's free for dinner next Thursday.

Now, you may notice something kind of familiar about these situations. I bet they remind you of instances where you would also want to be left alone. So, at the end of the day, use a little common sense. Ask yourself, if you were in the guy's shoes, would you want to be hit on at that moment? If the answer is no, then wait a bit. A better moment will come along. And if the answer is yes, then let's get to it!

Making Your Move

So . . . the guy you've been eyeing at the wedding all night is suddenly alone in the corner of the room, looking for someone to talk to. The moment is right to make your move.

The most important thing in the entire world is that when you go to talk to this guy, commit to it. Don't sneak up behind him with a pained look on your face like you're asking to borrow money. Walk over with confidence, flash him a big smile that he can't miss, and then strike up the conversation.

But wait! How do you start the conversation? Here's an example of what NOT to do:

You: Hi.

Guy: Hello.

You: I'm Susan.

Guy: I'm Rob.

You: So, what do you do, Rob?

Guy: I'm a lawyer.

You: Wow. Everyone I've met tonight has been a lawyer.

Guy: Yeah, well, there are a lot of us.

You: Which firm do you work for?

Guy: Rockwell & Tripp.

You: Really? That's impressive. Are you a partner?

Guy: Um . . . no. Not yet.

You: I once dated a guy from that firm. He drove the most ridiculously awesome Lexus.

Guy: I see.

You: Let's have a drink and talk about Rockwell & Tripp.

Guy: I don't think so.

I know, I know. You're laughing and thinking to yourself, "Come on, Janis. There's not a chance in China I would say *that*." Sure—you may not say everything in the above exchange. But at one point I bet you've said *something* from the above conversation. And let me guess: It was a disaster.

Just so we're all on the same page, here are the errors from the above example:

1. Don't ask him what he does. You're not a headhunter.

2. If he does tell you his occupation, don't insult the profession by saying something like "Everyone I've met tonight has been a lawyer."

3. Don't comment on his salary or his position at the firm/company where he works. It's *way* too personal for a first conversation and suggests you're interested in money more than love (which is a big concern for guys with dough).

4. Don't talk about former boyfriends (and how rich they were).

5. Don't come on to him too fast. It's slutty, not sexy.

6. Let him offer to buy you a drink, not the other way around.

So, let's go back and try that conversation again. It's a lot better if it goes like this:

You: They're playing "Desperado." Sort of a funny song for a wedding, huh?

Guy: Yeah. Maybe they're gonna play "You've Lost That Lovin' Feeling" next.

You: I'm Sarah. Friend of the bride's from college.

Guy: Hi Sarah. I'm Ted—the guy who's been beating the groom at basketball since childhood.

You: I love that tie you're wearing, Ted.

Guy: Oh, thank you! It's brand new and so far I've managed not to spill anything on it. But I haven't had any cake yet so there's still time for me to make a mess. Apparently there are two flavors—lemon and chocolate.

You: Really! I didn't see that there was lemon. That changes *everything*.

Guy: I like anyone who has zeal for lemon cake. Do you want to go have a taste test?

You: Great idea.

Needless to say, not every conversation is going to go this well. But if you keep certain things in mind, you're going to greatly increase your chances of walking away with a date:

1. It's okay to be funny. Men *love* this.

> *"Smart men appreciate smart and witty women. Go for it. If he's a dummy, you don't want him anyway."*
> —Ted, New York, NY

2. Introduce yourself near the beginning of the conversation. It's polite and it makes the conversation more relaxing because he won't be thinking, "I've been talking to this woman for twenty minutes and I still have no idea what her name is."

3. Don't be afraid to pay him a compliment. He's human. He'll love it.

> *"If a woman said she thought I looked handsome, I would be turned on and very approachable."*
>
> —Carl, Denver, CO

4. Have more than one topic of conversation. Talking about the wedding band was a cute way to get the ball rolling. But you don't want to get stuck on that topic forever. So move the conversation in a new direction when the time seems right. (Note: It's possible to go overboard here. While it's good to have two or three conversation topics, six is too many. And if he's really interested in talking about one particular topic, don't suddenly skip to something else. You'll seem like a whackadoodle.)

5. Go with the flow. Maybe you weren't planning to sit down and have a cake with him, but the fact that he wants to is a good sign. So go do it!

Of course, no matter how slick your social skills, there's going to be a little voice in the back of your mind that's wondering:

Is he really listening to me, or just checking out my body?

Let's cut to the chase. The answer is yes. The first time he meets you, he's going to be checking you out. Are you really surprised? And, for that matter, won't you be doing the same? Your appearance absolutely matters, and it matters a lot. No matter what the chemistry is between the two of you, if he's not attracted to you physically (and vice versa), you'll never get past the first date together.

And in case you're curious what he'll be checking out, I asked a bunch of my clients about which female body part their eyes go to first and here are the results:

Face: 50%
Butt: 33%
Breasts: 17%

So keep that in mind before you rush off and get breast implants (which I highly discourage anyway).

> *"If you're thinking about getting breast implants, think again! You may get more attention, but what kind of attention is it? Answer: the wrong kind!"*
>
> —Ted, New York, NY

The good news is that you don't have to be Heidi Klum in order to get a date. Seriously. Every guy has a wide range of women for which he thinks, "She's cute. Let me talk to her some more and see if she gets even cuter." Besides, if you really were a supermodel, he'd be too nervous to say anything to you except, "Wow, you're really . . . tall."

Before you get too stressed out about your appearance, remember that your personality will quickly become *crucial*.

As I already told you, men are very impressed if you have confidence when you approach them and a sense of humor when you talk to them. But those two characteristics are merely the tip of the iceberg. Here are two other traits that will factor heavily into a first impression:

♥ Intelligence. Whatever stereotype you think exists about guys only wanting to be with dumb hotties is wrong. Men may hook up with a moron, but they'll never seriously date a woman who isn't smart. I get so many guys who come back from a first date and tell me that they could never be attracted to the woman because she didn't have anything interesting to say.

♥ Politeness. Don't have a conversation with the guy while text messaging your friend about where you're going later that night. And if you answer your cell phone, it better be because your grandmother just won the lottery. Otherwise, you've just lost his interest forever.

> *"Do not check your phone. Turn it off."*
>
> —Adam, New York, NY

He Initiates Contact

Up to this point, I've been assuming that you were the one who's going to start the conversation. But, obviously, the old-fashioned way of him approaching you is always in vogue!

In those instances, the guy is the one who's got to pick the right moment and the right conversation topic, so the pressure is on him. But if you like him, there are a few things you can do to put him at ease:

Enthusiasm. If you're excited that he's come over and started talking to you, there's no need to play it cool and hide your feelings. Acting cold is only going to turn him away.

> *"If she likes me, she should be confident enough to show it."*
> —Will, Boston, MA

Discreetness. What I mean by this is that it's sometimes uncomfortable for a guy to hit on you in front of a group of your friends. So if he comes over and starts talking to you and you're interested, you can stand up and move the conversation to somewhere more private. It's a subtle act, but he'll be most appreciative.

Self control. You don't have to try to do too much. It's not necessary to show him that you can juggle, discuss food and wine, and dance the waltz. He's already interested in you. He doesn't need the full resume right now.

Be yourself. A guy who's come over to meet you wants to do just that. He wants to get to know *you*—not some freaky version of you that only comes out twice a year. So don't come across as a free-spirited outdoors type if that's not who you really are.

Once the two of you been chatting for a while and things seem to be going well, it's time to answer the question that every woman wants to know:

Is a guy okay with me asking for his phone number or e-mail the first time we meet? I mean, starting a conversation is one thing, but asking for his phone number—isn't that too aggressive?

Obviously, the ideal situation is to have him ask for your number. But if that doesn't happen, then go for it. Ask for his number. I feel like I've been saying this throughout the whole chapter, but I'm going to say it again—*men love a confident woman*. And nothing shows that better than you asking for his number. If he's thinking about asking for your number, he'll be excited to see that you're feeling the same way.

> *"If a woman asks for my number, I would be impressed with her confidence and consider it a plus."*
>
> —Carl, Denver, CO

The only thing you have to remember, of course, is that the guy may say no. But guess what—you'll survive. At least you don't have to go home wondering about what he would have said if you had only gotten up the courage to ask.

So, how should you ask for his number after you've been chatting for a while? Start with the subtle. For example, you could say:

- ♥ Should we continue this conversation later?
- ♥ Okay, I admit I have become unhealthily attached to my BlackBerry, but I just love e-mailing people with it. Can I have your e-mail address?
- ♥ This bar is right across the street from my office so I'm here with my coworkers all the time.

If he doesn't get the hint, nothing beats the direct route!

♥   We should get together sometime.

And if that still doesn't work, then you can try the RE-ALLY direct route:

♥   I'd like your phone number. Can you handle that?

Now, I know I've been emphasizing confidence, but, obviously, there can be a limit. At some point, confidence becomes aggression, which is a turn off to most men. So where do you draw the line? Well, it literally depends on *where* you are when you meet. If this is a guy you've just met at a bar or a wedding, he's going to assume that extreme aggressiveness on your part = an overwhelming need to get laid. Hey—he'll be happy to oblige, but he's not going to turn into your boyfriend. So show you're interested, but give him a chance to respond.

If, however, you're at a dinner party thrown by mutual friends and the setting is more personal and intimate, you have a lot more flexibility. You don't want to trap him in the corner and not let him move all night. But you're not perfect strangers, either, so it's no time to be shy. Let him know you're interested . . . otherwise, the window of opportunity may close.

If you're going to mess up, it's better to be slightly too aggressive than not aggressive enough. I'd rather you go down trying than never get in the game.

The Most Fabulous Category of Men

And now, ladies, a little treat for you to celebrate how much you've already learned. There's a creature out there more mythical than Bigfoot. He occupies your thoughts all the time. You think he might be the answer to all your prayers. That's right—I'm talking about the most fabulous category of men in the world: the diamond in the rough!

I classify a diamond in the rough as a guy you may skip over at first glance, but then, upon further review, he looks a lot more promising. With a little polishing he could really shine!

I know other people may have slightly different definitions, but I'm trying to be realistic and talk about the diamonds you're actually going to come across. I'm guessing there aren't a lot of strapping young cowboys showing up at your office Christmas party looking to date anyone who can use Microsoft Word.

How can you tell if a guy is a diamond in the rough?

Part of the charm of these guys is that they don't fit into the typical mold. But here are some traits to be on the lookout for:

1. He's very friendly. No matter how unusual his job, family, or clothing, a diamond in the rough will *always* be a very friendly, kind guy. If he's not, then, by definition, he's no diamond!

2. He's flattered when you come to talk to him. A diamond in the rough is usually not the sort of guy who has women constantly hitting on him, so he'll very much enjoy the attention.

3. He's quirky looking, but not unattractive. I bet you know what I mean by this, but in case you don't, flip

it around and think about your female friends. There's probably a woman you know who fits this description, and if you were telling a guy about her you'd say, "She has an unusual look, but I think it's very attractive."

4. He may be sitting alone, but he's comfortable. A diamond in the rough is a solid, content man (except for the fact that he hasn't met you yet). One of the ways you can spot this trait is to see if the guy is comfortable being by himself. I'm not saying he's antisocial. Rather, he's just the sort of guy who doesn't hyperventilate if he finds himself sitting alone for a bit.

5. He's taken care of his body. Finding a diamond in the rough is analogous to buying a house: You want the foundation and the roof to be good, but you're not going to walk away just because it needs a new coat of paint. If a guy has a bad haircut and is wearing a shirt with a hole, that can be fixed. If he has a scar across his face and his teeth are rotting, it may be time to run away and hide.

6. He's into you. The most important trait of all! Don't forget it!

Okay . . . I know there's a lot of information in this chapter, so let me take a second to summarize everything I've written.

What this chapter really boils down to is how to flirt:

How to Flirt with a Guy

♥   Tell him your name—always a good place to start!

♥   Be funny. Humor is a big turn on for all guys.

♥   Show off your intelligence. Guys will sleep with dumb
     blondes, but they're not going to marry one.

♥   Be confident. If you've made up your mind to flirt with
     a guy, commit to it. Otherwise it's REALLY awkward.

♥   Be polite. Don't force yourself into a conversation he's
     having with someone else.

♥   Pay him a compliment. Flattery will get you everywhere!

♥   Be yourself. The most important thing of all. He wants
     to get a sense of who you are. If you're sarcastic one
     meeting and then irony-free the next, he's going to
     think you have multiple personality disorder.

And, just to be sure we're crystal clear, here's what NOT to
do:

How NOT to Flirt with a Guy

   Talk dirty. It's cheap and slutty, not sexy.

   Ask him a question and then not listen to his answer.

🖓   Be overly obsessed with what he does or how much
     money he makes.

🖓   Have only one topic of conversation.

🖓   Complain.

Not What You're After

Be careful about a guy you've just met who asks all the right questions in a conversation . . . but doesn't seem to be listening to your answers at all. That's a big warning sign of a shark.

Obviously, if you're in a noisy, crowded bar, there's going to be lots of distractions and he may not catch every word you say. But some guys will actually turn away when you're talking and watch the baseball game, gesture to a friend, or just stare aimlessly at a wall. You think they're not interested, except that when you stop talking they turn back and suddenly ask you another question.

Don't fall for that trick. If a guy is really interested in you, he'll want to hear what you have to say.

On the flip side, you should also be careful about guys who never let you speak at all. If he spends the night talking nonstop about himself, watch out! He's probably insecure, egotistical, or both. And either way . . . you can do better.

> *"Men who talk only about themselves are easy eliminates."*
>
> —Adam, New York, NY

I couldn't have said it better.

Let Him Down Easy

You approach the guy. You chat with the guy. And then you realize he's not the one for you. Maybe the chemistry isn't there. Maybe he's not as attractive up close. Maybe he's drinking way too much. Whatever the case, you know for certain that you won't be going out with him. Hey, it happens.

But, ladies, please do not sit and talk with this guy all night if you have no interest in going out with him. You don't want to be rude, but, at the same time, you don't owe this guy anything. At the first break in the conversation, say something like, "I should be getting back to my friends. Nice talking with you." Grab your drink and be on your way.

Let somebody else have a crack at the guy—perhaps their chemistry with him will be better.

CHAPTER 3

The Rendezvous Strategy
The First Phone Call

Okay, so you've met a guy who seems promising. You chatted for a bit, had some laughs, and exchanged phone numbers. Now, the moment of truth: Will there be a date?

You already know the first topic I'm going to discuss, don't you? After all, you're a single woman, and at some point in your dating life, you've wondered the following:

Can I call the guy or should I wait for him to call me?

I ALWAYS tell women the same thing: Call him. *You've got nothing to lose.* The long and the short of it is that we're right back at the confidence issue. If a guy's into you, he will be impressed that you had the balls to call him. Men LOVE that you know what you want and you're taking control. On a scale of one to ten, he'll think you're a twenty-five.

Now, I know the skeptics out there will say:

Um, Janis . . . maybe he's not calling because he changed his mind and doesn't want to go out!

Sure, that could be the case. But who cares? You should still call him if you want to go out. If he turns you down, you'll survive. But the fact that he gave you his number in the first place means he's interested, so I think you have a very good chance of getting a date if you call.

If you decide to wait for him to call, you should know that *he'll do it in the first twenty-four to forty-eight hours after he gets your number*. Any longer than that, and you probably won't be hearing from him at all.

The idea that men like to play it cool and wait a week before calling is just not true. Or, at least, it's not true *anymore*. It's classic behavior from a twenty-three-year-old dude. But when a guy gets into his late twenties and thirties, he's not going to beat around the bush. He may wait a day or two, but waiting a week is just juvenile.

Now, obviously, it's a case-by-case situation. But in the age of cell phones, a guy can call you from anywhere at anytime. It doesn't matter if he's traveling or having a busy day at work. If he likes you, he'll call, and he'll do it quickly.

But let me say again that I've seen this telephone waiting game drive women crazy. So even if you start out waiting for him to call, it's still okay to pick up the phone and give him a ring if you're getting impatient. You've got nothing to lose. Call him!

I'm So Glad You Called

The good news, as I said earlier, is that if a guy is brave enough to ask for your number when he meets you (and lucky enough to get it), he's going to want to go out on a date with you.

So now let's say you've called him or he's called you and you're on the phone together. This phone conversation is pretty important, to say the least. If you guys have a weird chat, it could destroy all the momentum.

What's he looking for during this first phone conversation? Lots of things:

♥ Excitement from you. This is *crucial*. It's not too late for him to change his mind if he's worried you're just going through the motions with him. So even if you're having a bad day and you're exhausted, it's worth doing a little acting job and putting on a happy face.

And, for the love of God, don't yell at him for not calling you sooner! Yikes! He'll hang up faster than me with a telemarketer. If you waited for him to call and can't get over how long it took, then just tell him you don't want to go out and hang up.

♥ Your phone voice. Don't be slutty or cheap. Even if the guy's already met you, your tone of voice on the phone goes a long way in making him very excited (or very scared) about having dinner with you. You don't want to have a phone sex voice (slutty) and you don't want to swear like a longshoreman (cheap).

♥ His phone voice. If you haven't met the guy before, don't judge a book by its cover. Here's what I mean: I set up one of my clients, Daniel, with a woman I just absolutely knew he'd be perfect with. Her name was Amanda, and she was a friggin' knockout: the brains, the body, the personality—she had it all. But when Amanda talked to Daniel on the phone, she suddenly got scared away by his nasally voice. Daniel wasn't trying to sound weird—

that's just how he speaks, okay? Anyway, Amanda got so freaked out that she decided she didn't want to go out with Daniel. Cut to three months later, they're both at the same dinner party and Amanda is flirting with Daniel for half the night before she puts together that it was the guy I was trying to set her up with! In real life, his voice didn't bother her at all. But she overanalyzed a meaningless detail before she ever met him and it could have wound up costing her . . . BIG TIME!

♥ Your undivided attention. Even if he's caught you at a hectic moment, try your best to talk to him, *and only him*. If things are really bonkers, you can ask to call him back, but be sure you do it ASAP. If you say five minutes and call him back three hours later, the date will be over before it starts.

♥ A little casual chit-chat. This is a nice cherry on top of the sundae, but keep it brief! You're not on the date yet. Save the long, involved (and flirtatious!) conversation for when you're face to face. For now, keep it friendly, but keep it brief.

♥ Information on your availability. You need to walk a fine line here. Don't try to squeeze him in when you're not really available because he'll be annoyed that he doesn't have your complete attention. But—and this is really important—nothing flatters a guy more than having you rearrange your schedule a bit to make room for him. Even freeing up an hour or two for drinks sends the message that you're really excited to spend some time with him.

I just had this happen to a client of mine named Ken. He was trying to set up a first date with a woman named Mary. Mary has a very high powered job in New York and her schedule is total chaos. But she had met Ken previously and was very excited about seeing him. Mary cancelled two meetings so that she could have a cocktail with Ken two days after he called. Suffice to say, Ken was flattered and the date got off on the right foot before it even started.

Now, if you can't free up an hour or two in the next couple of days, you need to at least try to come up with a night in the next week when you're free. Unless you're out of town, if you tell him you're busy every night for the next week, he'll think you're saying that you don't want to go out with him (even if that's not the case). If you really are that busy, you have to try to move some plans around to make time for the date.

Warning

Don't overdo it when it comes to your availability, though. If you tell him, "I'm free every night this week and every night next week," he may wonder why you have no plans. As a client told me:

> *"Do not be available all the time. This surprisingly works even though men know that you do it."*
> —Adam, New York, NY

Now, please don't take that warning too far and assume that I'm advocating mind games. I'm not. Men like a little challenge . . . but they hate games and manipulation.

At this point, I think I need to take a minute and discuss *The Rules*. For those of you who don't know, *The Rules* is a well-known dating book that basically advocates a manipulative approach to dating.

I'm not generally in the habit of dissing other dating books. But the problem I have with *The Rules* is that all of my clients disagree with everything in it (needless to say, I feel the same way)! Now, some would say that men are just upset because women are finally beating them at their own game.

But read that last sentence again and you'll see how ridiculous that whole philosophy is. If you approach dating as a game that one of you has to win by beating the other person, *you are never going to be happy*. NEVER! A relationship can't be a competition if it's going to last forever. The perfect mate is someone you can relax and be yourself around. You can't play a game for fifty years of marriage. It's never going to work and you're going to wind up getting a divorce.

Yes, there are some guys out there who may get off on being manipulated. But you don't want them. Trust me. The vast majority of guys approach dating very simply: If I like the girl, I'll go out with her. If I don't, I won't.

> *"Remember, we're men. We're not that complicated."*
> —Charlie, New York, NY

It's only a small percentage of guys who are into manipulation, and they give the other 95 percent of men a bad name. So don't alter your behavior in hopes of attracting a small minority of men that you don't want to be with anyway!

A Man, a Plan

Obviously, the most important part of the conversation is to actually make plans. There are three ways this usually plays out:

Situation #1: You Have the Power In this scenario, the guy calls to ask you out for dinner or drinks and he wants your input. What should you do? Well, for starters, don't pick the most expensive restaurant in town, even if you're dying to try it. It sends the message that his wealth is the only thing that's important. And, frankly, he might not be that wealthy, which puts him in a very awkward position.

I know you want true love and *you* know you want true love, but you have to let *the guy* know that too.

> *"Why do so many women almost always demand that the first date be at an expensive restaurant? Too often I hear, 'I've been there, how about the five star choice?' Some women treat the guy as though he's only there to buy dinner."*
>
> —Nick, San Francisco, CA

The Four Seasons will have to wait for a different occasion. Instead, pick a nice-but-not-too-nice neighborhood place that you know and love. If you pick a place you're familiar with, it's one less thing to worry about.

If you don't have a place you love, use the *Zagat* guide or City Search or the local dining magazine for your area to get ideas. Or, even better, ask a friend for a place they've used for a first date.

Situation #2: Choose Your Own Adventure In this scenario, the guy gives you several options of what you can do on the date and wants your help deciding. You could meet for a drink after work, or there's a casual Italian place in his neighborhood where you could go for dinner, or maybe both.

If the guy calls you with a choice, you must be decisive. Don't get into a passive-aggressive "I'll do whatever you want to do" battle. Yuck. Those conversations take forever and nothing ever gets accomplished. He's asking you for your opinion. So go ahead and give it.

It's also important not to reject all of his choices. It's sweet that he's giving you options, so don't make him regret that decision by telling him all of the places sound lousy.

Even if none of the choices are ones you yourself would have picked, give him the benefit of the doubt and roll with it. If it's a terrible restaurant or an awkwardly crowded bar, let that factor into whether he deserves a second date with you. But for now, give him a chance to try to impress you.

Situation #3: He's Made the Plan A lot of the time, the guy will have an itinerary for the evening all planned out and is merely seeking your approval. Which leads to the following question:

Can I object to his plans without hurting his feelings?

It depends. There are good reasons and bad reasons to object to his plans. To help you understand exactly what I'm talking about, take a look at the following chart:

Good Reasons to Object to His Plans for the First Date	Bad Reasons to Object to His Plans for the First Date
You have a food allergy (coconut milk) and he's recommended a restaurant that's sure to make you sick (Bangkok Palace).	The restaurant he picked isn't as fancy as you'd hoped.
He wants to go to a movie that you've already seen.	He picked a movie that you kinda told your friend Stephanie that you'd maybe try to see with her.
He's picked a bar that you go to all the time, and so you know that they're having live music there that night, which might make it tough to talk to each other.	Just drinks? No dinner? What's the deal?!
He's picked a restaurant that you happen to have just gone to twice in the past week.	He picked a restaurant that you've never heard of.

Needless to say, these are just some examples, but you get the idea:

DON'T OBJECT TO HIS PLANS UNLESS YOU REALLY HAVE TO.

This isn't some sort of sexist "men are always right" rule. We're just talking about simple courtesy here, okay? When someone extends you an invitation, the polite thing to do is to accept the offer without conditions. If you say, "Well, can we go for French instead of Italian?" or "That place is too far from my home," you'll come across as high maintenance.

> *"There's a fine line between knowing what you want and having to get your way."*
>
> —Adam, New York, NY

If the relationship lasts, there will be plenty of moments when you can be the one making the plans. But for now, go with his itinerary if you possibly can.

Change of Plans

And now, ladies, it's time for the most important piece of advice I'll give you in this whole chapter:

ONCE YOU MAKE PLANS, DON'T KEEP CHANGING THEM.

This drives guys friggin' INSANE. I can't tell you how many times I've set a guy up with a woman who I think is absolutely perfect for him . . . only to have the whole thing fall apart because she keeps canceling on him. I'll say, "She's perfect for you!" and he'll say, "Janis, I don't care! If she has this much trouble picking a time for the first date, I don't know how we'd ever get anything done as a couple."

And there you have it, ladies. You could be the most perfect match in the whole world for a guy, and it won't matter if you keep changing the plans for the first date.

Okay, okay. I hear your objections. Whenever I give a speech about this topic, some nice, smart woman raises her hand and asks:

But what if my grandmother becomes ill? Can't I reschedule the date then?

Of course! Any guy will understand if a serious conflict comes up. Just remember to *call him as soon as possible*. If, God forbid, there is a family emergency I know your first phone call isn't going to be to the guy you have a date with this weekend. But you should call the guy before 7:15 p.m. on Friday night. If you call him as soon as you can, he'll understand and be glad to reschedule. And, by the way, it goes without saying that you should extend the same courtesy to him if he calls you with an equally legitimate reason for having to reschedule.

On the other hand, if you flake out and call him the day of the date, he'll think you're blowing him off. He won't want to reschedule—especially if we're talking about something less serious than an ill relative. If you have an unavoidable work conflict and have to go to Des Moines immediately, that's fine. But, um, hello, they have phones in Iowa. Just because you're out of town doesn't mean you get a free pass on being a ditz.

Even worse is simply forgetting the date altogether. This is unacceptable.

> *"The worst excuse I've gotten for having to reschedule a date was from a woman who said she 'forgot.' I was looking for someone intelligent, so that was sort of a deal breaker."*
>
> —Brad, Dallas, TX

Also remember that you *don't* have an unlimited number of times to reschedule. After about two postponements—no

matter how legit—he's going to lose interest. If that seems unfair, let me point out that most of the time when women postpone dates (or "forget" to go on them), it isn't because of a
family emergency; it's because of a lame reason like one of the
following:

Lame Excuses for Postponing a First Date

Excuse: I'm tired.

Janis says: So . . . go get some sleep!

Excuse: My friends are all getting together that night.

Janis says: How many times have you been out with
these friends? Three hundred and forty-two?
They'll be getting together again soon. You
can miss this one occasion.

Excuse: I have a lot of work.

Janis says: Everyone has a lot of work. Work late the
other nights so you can go out on a date.

Excuse: I'm not feeling well.

Janis says: This is fine if you have the flu, but 98 percent
of the time, this excuse is synonymous with
"I'm tired." And you see what I had to say
about that!

If you find yourself using these excuses, ladies, it probably
means you have some issues. You need to prioritize dating if
you want to be in a great relationship. If you're constantly saying you don't want to go out, you're just fooling yourself. The
guy isn't the problem. You are.

Look, I know you're nervous about dating, but that's okay.
A lot of guys are nervous too. Seriously! Many of my clients

are captains of industry who have conquered their chosen profession and yet, when it comes to a first date, they're as nervous as a deer. I'm ALWAYS giving them verbal and emotional support. And now I'm doing the same for you.

As nervous as these guys get, though, they ultimately decide to be bold and go on a date. And they want to see you doing the same thing. Instead of making excuses why you can't go out, start using this excuse with your friends: "Sorry, ladies, I can't have dinner tomorrow night. I have a date."

A Word on Snooping

You obviously want to know the guy you're going out with. But it's possible to know too much. What do I mean by that? Well, when I set my clients up on a date, I don't tell the woman the guy's last name. Why? Because the first thing that woman will do is go on the Internet and Google the guy.

This can be really dangerous.

For starters, women always try to find a picture of the guy on the Internet. Inevitably, if there is a picture, it's terrible. It's usually out of date or very corporate looking, which is not a good representation of what the guy looks like now. Obviously, men do this as well, with equally misleading results.

But women tend to take it a step further than men. If the guy is well known in the community—he's a high profile attorney or doctor, let's say—then many women will read all about the guy before the date. It's nice to show you're interested, but it can also feel like you're a stalker. And if the guy happens to be very successful, he'll worry that what you're really reading about is his large income.

Snooping also suggests obsessive behavior on your part,

which is NOT a good way to approach a new person. A lot of men will be freaked out if they find out you've been Googling them obsessively. I mean . . . it's weird and suggests you spend too much time on your computer and not enough time with other people.

Bottom line: You can do a little research, but don't go over the top. You want to start every date with an open mind, but if you've done too much snooping around, it will be impossible to separate reality from reputation.

Let me do what I did last chapter and summarize everything I've written here by giving you a quick reference guide for how to schedule a first date:

How to Schedule a First Date

♥   Call him! You've got nothing to lose . . . even if he says no.

♥   Be available! Make dating a priority. Cancel other plans if you have to.

♥   Be excited—so simple, but so important!

♥   Go with the flow. If he's planned the evening, go along with it. If his plan is a disaster, you can hold that against him after the date . . . but not before. (And more often than not, he'll plan a great evening.)

As with flirting, sometimes knowing how NOT to schedule a first date is just as valuable:

How NOT to Schedule a First Date

 Use a phone sex voice.

 Put him on hold while you're on the phone.

 Insist on the most expensive restaurant in town.

 Keep rescheduling the night you want to go out.

 Snoop around on the Internet for gossip and/or facts about the guy.

The Over-Dater

Ladies, here's something very important to keep in mind: Don't schedule too many dates in a row. I know that sounds weird coming from me because I LOVE setting people up on dates. And if you're serious about finding a guy, I'm all for an aggressive dating schedule.

But let's say you have a great date with a guy on Friday, and you wind up making out with him at the end of it. Can you blame the guy for being hurt when he learns that you'll be out with a different guy on Saturday night?

You need to build into your weekend plans the possibility that the Friday date could work out. Otherwise, the guy will feel sucker-punched.

I know what you're thinking:

Well, why does he have to know about the date on Saturday? Can't I just lie to him?

Guess what my answer is? NO! YOU CAN'T JUST LIE TO HIM! That's even worse. Somehow, someway, he'll find out you lied—because they always do—and now you've insulted him twice.

Aggressive dating is good. But one first date per weekend will makes things a lot easier on everyone.

Not What You're After

Here's something that you should definitely be on the lookout for: the guy who hasn't made any effort in planning the first date. Now, I know what you're saying:

Janis, didn't one of the scenarios you described in this chapter involve the guy asking my input about the first date? Is that something to worry about?

Look, I think it's great when a guy wants to get your thoughts before planning the evening. But what I'm talking about here is the guy who calls you and has done no thinking about the date whatsoever. Lunch? Dinner? Drinks? Coffee? Who knows?! Well, your date should! He's got to be ready with some ideas even if he's asking for your input. He shouldn't be calling up and saying, "I dunno. What do you want to do?"

A man should take charge and have a plan. I have a client, Eddie, who spends hours planning a first date. He researches restaurants. He picks locations that are convenient for his date. He even scouts out places in person if he's never been there before. And when I ask him why he's so obsessive-compulsive, he says, "Janis, you never know. This woman could wind up being my future wife!"

Needless to say, I LOVE that attitude. And even if every guy out there isn't as thorough as Eddie, they should have a similar mentality. Their life could change after their date with you. So they better make it count!

Getting ideas from you is considerate. Leaving the whole thing up to you means he's a man without a plan, and that's a very bad sign.

Let Him Down Easy

Sometimes you've given a guy your number, and then, thinking about it later, you kind of wish you hadn't. Naturally, that guy will *always* call for a date (Murphy's Law!). So what should you do?

Well, as I've already said, I think just about any guy is worth one date, because you never know . . . he could really surprise you. And you're never going to find true love sitting on your sofa!

But if you really don't want to go, you should tell him so and not just leave him twisting in the wind. He's interested in finding love too, and if you're not the one, you should tell him ASAP so he can move on and make some other single woman happy.

Obviously, if he never calls in the first place, you're off the hook. But if he leaves you a message, you should definitely get back to him. Send him an e-mail or, if you don't have his e-mail address, give him a call.

Now, if telling him point blank, "I changed my mind!" seems too harsh, then this is one occasion where you're allowed to tell him a little fib. If you say that you've started seeing someone else, it will do the trick. It's not even that much of a white lie—the truth is that there *are* other guys out there you have your eye on. In any event, the problem is solved. No guy wants to be part of a love triangle, so he'll quickly move on to someone else as well. You've let him down easy, and acted very classy in the process. Nice work!

CHAPTER 4

I'll Pick You Up at Seven
The First Date

There is absolutely nothing more exciting than a first date! It's the key moment in every relationship. When you wind up with someone, you always remember your first date.

So let's go through the night chronologically and examine what thoughts are going to be running through the guy's mind every step of the way.

Getting Ready

Here's a question I get asked all the time from women:

Janis, when I have a first date, I usually spend all day stressing about the details of what I'm going to wear—things like my earrings, shoes, and handbag. But, seriously, does a guy care about stuff like this? Isn't he just going to notice my face and my breasts?

Your face and your breasts may be the first thing he notices, but over the course of the night, he's going to check out everything you have on. Now, unless your date is Ralph Lauren, he's probably not going to obsess over the details as much as you do. So you don't have to have a meltdown if your favorite handbag has a hole in it. Your second favorite handbag is still going to look great as far as he's concerned.

That said, your date is not totally naïve when it comes to fashion. He wants to see you looking your best. Just as you hope he doesn't show up smelling like the gym, so too will he notice if you put your best foot forward. This doesn't mean you have to run out and get a Chanel suit and a face-lift; it does mean you should select an outfit that differs from the one you wear to walk your dog.

> "Every woman has something that's great about her physically. If you've got legs, get 'em out there and don't cover them up. Always show off your best asset—albeit tastefully."
>
> —Ted, New York, NY

Let me take that quote from Ted one step further: There's no need to call attention to the assets you *don't* love. If your date tells you that you have beautiful eyes, don't respond by saying, "Yeah, but I wish my hips were thinner." If you do that, guess what he'll be looking at the rest of the night?

Now that you're a bit more relaxed about your general fashion requirements for the first date (remember: it's not a runway show in Milan), let's talk about a few specifics:

Makeup. It's nice to wear a little bit, to show that this evening is a special occasion. But men would always prefer that you err on the side of too little makeup rather than too much. If you go over the top, guys feel like they aren't getting an accurate view of what you really look like. And they assume this is because you have something to hide.

> *"A don't for women in dating: too much makeup, [because] then I imagine 'wow, I bet she looks rough in the morning.'"*
>
> —Matt, Washington, D.C.

Hair. Get a blowout! Your hair is one of the first things a guy will notice because, hello, it's right at eye level. So take the time to do it right. No ponytails. No frizzy disasters. Wear your hair down. You want him to be fantasizing about running his fingers through it. And that's not going to be happening if your hair hasn't been given some tender love and care.

If you don't have time to do it yourself, go to a salon and have it done right. In fact, even if you do have the time to do it yourself, you should go to a salon and have it done right! No, you don't need a blowout every time you see him for the rest of eternity. But for the first date: *absolutely!*

Straight from Work. It sounds incredible, but some women think it's a good idea to wear their work outfits on a date. They tell me:

It's the twenty-first century, Janis. You can wear hip clothes to work!

I don't care! Even if your job allows you to wear sexy clothes (which I seriously doubt), they're not going to look fresh after you've had them on all day. Wrinkles, sweat stains, the smell of coffee—all of these factors can wreak havoc on your best laid fashion plans.

> *"Don't come straight from work. For God's sake go home and start over from scratch if you are seeing me. I will be."*
> —Evan, Seattle, WA

Even if you're meeting him at a place around the corner from where you work, you should allow yourself some time to run home and freshen up. And if that's not possible, at least bring a change of clothes to the office.

Skirt versus pants. I said earlier that guys may not notice as many fashion details as you do, but they'll certainly notice *some* of them. For example, if you're going to a five star restaurant and he shows up in a suit, you do *not* want to show up in jeans (even if they're your awesome pair of jeans that totally make your butt look amazing!).

Men almost always prefer that you wear a skirt instead of pants (especially if you have killer legs!). Jeans are probably going to be too casual, and "nice pants" feel too much like you're wearing business casual attire on a date. Men constantly tell me that they want their date to dress and look *feminine*. That's the buzzword. So wear a skirt. It's sexy. It's festive. And it shows you put some thought into the date.

> *"Match what you wear to the restaurant. If it's a nice place, then a little black dress works. In fact, a little black dress always works anywhere."*
> —Ted, New York, NY

Here's how I'd recommend matching what you wear to the restaurant:

Venue	Janis Recommends	And Whatever You Do, Don't
A casual, neighborhood bistro	Simple skirt and a sweater	Wear sneakers
The country club	A blazer and a conservative skirt	Show too much cleavage
Ultra-hip place that serves tiny plates of food that you share	Your trendiest skirt and an attention-grabbing top	Be bland
One of the city's ten best restaurants	High fashion: a beautiful skirt, heels (or boots), an elegant top, and your favorite necklace/earrings	Wear an $8 sweater from The Gap over a top that costs ten times as much
The greatest burger shack in the world	Something that looks good with mustard spilled on it!	Wear something that *already* has mustard stains on it

If you're not sure of the fanciness of your date location, do a little research: Look up the place on the Internet, ask a friend who has been there, or call the restaurant itself. Needless to say, a male bartender at the restaurant probably won't have the first clue as to what you should wear. However, he'll be happy to let you know if it's the kind of place that carves roast duck tableside, or if it's the kind of place where you pound blue crabs with your own mallet. That should be all the data you need.

Warning!

Don't dress too slutty here. Yes, you want to arouse his interest, but he's also got to feel like you could be the mother of his children. If your shirt is unbuttoned too much, he may want to sleep with you, but he's not sure he wants to date you.

I had a client, Andrew, who was meeting his date, Wanda, at a beachfront restaurant in the Hamptons. It was a casual restaurant and it was summertime, so Andrew wasn't expecting Wanda to be dressed formally. But let's just say that Wanda went a little too far in the other direction. Her shirt was so low cut that you could see 95 percent of her bra . . . and her nipples were just barely out of sight. All Andrew (or anyone else in the restaurant) could focus on was whether Wanda was going to pop out of that shirt. She didn't, but by then it was a lost cause. Andrew was done with Wanda.

Here's another tip: If you've met your date before, *wear something different from what you had on the night you guys met.* A lot of ladies think:

Well, he liked me in that outfit enough to ask me out, so I should wear it again to ensure that he'll love how I look.

WRONG! He probably has a mental picture of you from that night. If you show up in the same outfit, he's going to think you're an even lazier dresser than he is (and that's not a compliment, even coming from a laid back guy). If you can't remember what you wore the night you guys met, play it safe and go buy something new. Again, I'm not talking about a $500 dress—a new sweater will go a long way.

The bottom line is not to get too stressed out about your outfit. If you spend the whole evening fussing over your clothes—or anything, for that matter—it's a BIG TIME turnoff for men.

So don't wear something that's so tight you can't eat in it (even if it makes your waist look tiny). Remember that stomachs expand after a meal. If you wear something that feels sexy and comfortable, you'll be relaxed, which will make your date relaxed—and that's the name of the game.

The Date Begins

Enough preparation—let's get on with the evening. There are two ways the date can typically begin:

Option #1: He Wants to Pick You Up.

Ladies, even if you feel like this is an unnecessary gesture, let him do it. From a practical point of view, this ensures that you won't have any trouble finding the restaurant (or, if you do, at least you're already together).

But it's also MUCH more romantic if he wants to pick you up. It's a good sign if he wants the evening to have a certain formality to it. You're not just going out to the movie with some friends; you're having dinner with him. It's a special night and he wants to show you that by making the effort to come by and pick you up. So let him!

When he shows up at your place, he's looking to give you a kiss on the cheek. Take it in stride. You can expect one kiss if he's American, two if he's English or French, and at least seven if he's Italian.

We've now reached a moment in the evening where many women make a common mistake:

*He came all this way to pick me up, so the least I can do is in-
vite him in, right?*

No—it's not necessary. A guy wants to save a tour of your
apartment as a reward for later. He'd rather see the place
when the two of you don't have to rush off to dinner. Or, to
put it another way, he wants to come in when he's invited to
stay for a while . . .

One big caveat here: If you don't know the guy particularly
well (i.e., you met on the Internet) and you aren't totally comfortable giving him your home address, then don't. DON'T
EVER DO ANYTHING THAT MAKES YOU UNCOMFOR-
TABLE! Just politely tell him that it's easier for you to meet
him somewhere. He'll completely understand. And if he
doesn't, then good-bye to him.

Option #2: Meeting Him at the Restaurant

Sometimes, meeting up at the restaurant may just be more
practical, so you don't need to hit the panic button just because your date suggests doing things this way. If he doesn't
offer to pick you up, don't insist—it makes you look high-
maintenance and it makes him feel like he's already done
something hideously wrong.

The downside to this option, though, is that there could be
some serious miscommunication. To avoid that disaster, here
are four things guys hope you will do:

1. Be on time. You're allowed a ten minute grace period.
   That's it! A lot of women tell me that they want to be
   "fashionably late." You can be fashionably late when
   you're showing up to your best friend's dinner party.
   But on a first date . . . forget it! Neither of you have

earned that right yet. There's nothing fashionable about being late on a first date—it's just RUDE! Trust me!

> *"One of the worst things is meeting people who are unreliable. Things like being unreasonably late make it hard to stay positive and enthusiastic about someone."*
>
> —Marco, Miami, FL

2. If you're going to be later than ten minutes you'd better (a) call and (b) have a good reason (and I mean VERY good!).

3. If you get there first, don't sit down at the bar and start drinking alone. Your date will want to join you for the first drink of the evening (and pay for it). If sitting at the bar makes you more relaxed while you wait, order a glass of water or a club soda.

4. Check in with the hostess before you disappear anywhere. If you tell the hostess that you're meeting Mr. Name-of-Your-Date and that you'll be waiting for him at the bar, it makes things run much smoother when he does arrive. The hostess can point you out or describe what you're wearing. This helps avoid the awkward situation of him trying to pick you out of a crowd.

By the way, not every first date is going to be at a restaurant. I always encourage my clients to choose dinner because it's familiar, it's social, and it gives the evening a nice structure. But some men prefer an activity that's a little less time intensive and/or expensive for a first date. That's okay. But even if you're meeting for drinks or coffee or lunch, the same rules apply: Dress appropriately for the occasion, be on time, and don't start slurping down martinis (or lattes) without him.

Cocktails

Once the two of you are at the restaurant together, one of the first things your date probably will ask is if you'd like to join him for a cocktail. If there's a slight wait for the table, you'll have the drink at the bar. If not, you'll order at the table. Either way: *Be careful with the booze*!

It's rude to turn down his offer to buy you a drink. That sets an inhospitable tone for the night and no guy wants to date a prude. If you're worried about your alcohol tolerance, you can take all night to get through your martini or glass of wine.

Plus, it's true what they say about alcohol having a calming effect on people. Even the most relaxed person could usually use a little nip.

Now, if you don't drink at all, that's fine—just tell him up front. If it freaks him out that you're dry, he's just going to have to accept that if he wants to be with you.

But if you do decide to have a drink with him, whatever you do, DON'T GET DRUNK! Contrary to popular belief, guys do not want you to get tanked so that you'll be more willing to go to bed with them. Men want to see that you can enjoy a drink socially but still remain in control.

> *"We don't want the mother of our kids spilling her wine and slurring her words on a first date."*
>
> —Adam, New York, NY

Sometimes, though, you may get drunk accidentally:

STORY TIME

One of my clients, Les, went out to dinner with a woman named Molly. They had a cocktail before dinner and then a bottle of wine with dinner. Molly doesn't weigh very much and so she wanted to avoid drinking a lot because she had a low tolerance. But Les kept refilling her wine glass all night long, and she thought it would be rude if she didn't keep drinking. Well, the long and the short of it is that Molly got TANKED, and then, in a drunken stupor, insulted Les's clothes. Can you believe it? She actually made fun of his outfit to his face. Needles to say, they never went out again.

Yes, Les was the one who kept refilling Molly's wine glass, but guys assume you know your own tolerance. Don't be afraid to cut yourself off, even if you're drinking an expensive bottle of wine. Better to put a cork in the bottle and take it home than to stumble out of the restaurant.

The Menu

This is the moment in the night where some women tend to go insane and overanalyze the entrée choice into oblivion.

Have you ever caught yourself thinking the following:

- ♥ Will he think that I'm indulgent/spoiled/likely-to-get-fat-one-day if I order anything other than a salad and fish?
- ♥ Should I let him order for me? What if he picks something I don't like?
- ♥ Will he be upset if I get one of the more expensive entrées, like filet mignon, even if it's what I really want?

The ordering of the meal is a very important moment in the night. But it's not for the reasons you think. What you order is actually much less important to men than *how* you order it. Specifically, your dates wants you to . . .

Be nice to the waiter. This is the first thing guys will be on the lookout for when you order. In fact, this rule doesn't just apply to waiters. You should also be courteous to busboys, taxi drivers, your doorman—anyone you come in contact with. A confident, happy person will never be rude to someone just because they happen to work in a service-oriented job. If you're mean to the waiter, your date will immediately start thinking about how you'll treat him if he ever messes something up, and the evening will be OVER!

> *"Do not be rude to waiters, taxi drivers, or anyone else. Good rule for life and it will kill you on a date."*
> —Brian, Chicago, IL

Be decisive. Men don't like it when they have to make every decision for you. So don't ask him to pick what you should have for dinner. If he's been to the restaurant before, it's perfectly fine to ask him for a recommendation. But when the waiter arrives, make your own decision.

And, for the love of God, don't hem and haw for ten minutes about what you'll be having while the waiter is standing there beside you. You're an adult. Make a decision and stand by it. If you can't pick out something as simple as a dinner entrée, your date will immediately start worrying that you'll need six weeks to decide if you want to kiss him. It's beyond annoying!

Be satisfied. In truth, what men care about more than anything else is that you enjoy the meal. He picked the restaurant and he's hoping you'll like it. He'd rather see you eating something you love than picking at something you hate. If he has to watch you push food around your plate, he'll feel like he selected a bad spot, which could be enough to make him uncomfortable for the rest of the evening. Not good. So order something you really want to eat and then enjoy it.

Frankly, ladies, having a healthy appetite is SEXY! Taste is one of the five senses, and if you're in touch with that part of your body, your date will start to wonder what else you're sensual about.

> *"A date from hell is where she can't find anything she likes and starts asking if the chef can make something [not on the menu]. So now she's ordered two or three items but only picks at them because she's on a diet and 'only wanted to taste it.'"*
>
> —Nick, San Francisco, CA

Also, for the record, a guy *will notice* if you order the most expensive entrée or bottle of wine on the menu. Some guys will get more annoyed by this than others. Here's the best way to play it safe: Ask him what he's having and let that be your price guide. If he's selecting an entrée that costs $22, then it's fine for you to get one that costs $25 . . . but hold off on the one that costs $44. (You don't need to ask him permission, though. He's not your dad, and you're not six years old.)

As for wine, the odds are high that he'll want to pick something out so that he can show off his knowledge of all things vino. If he asks you to select a bottle, it's polite to go with something that's not too expensive. It doesn't have to be the cheapest one, but make it something in the lower end of the price range.

If he does ask for your opinion on the wine, many women think it's a good solution to ask the waiter for a recommendation. You still need to be careful, though. You should mention that you want something simple that will go with what you ordered. You don't want the waiter to recommend a $200 bottle of wine, which then puts your date in the awkward position of looking cheap when he asks for a less expensive option.

And one last thing: Don't insist on bottled water. I was having dinner with one of my clients in Los Angeles, Jay, and we were talking about what sort of things drive him crazy on a first date. Jay's a great guy—very funny, very outgoing—and while we were talking, the waiter asked whether we wanted bottled water or tap water. And Jay's eyes suddenly lit up. "Tap is fine," he said. Then he turned to me and said, "Janis, why do some women insist on ordering bottled water? Tap water is perfectly fine. There's no need to run up the tab by getting bottled water."

Now, if the date is in Mexico and you're worried about getting sick from the tap, then fine—you can order bottled water. But I'm guessing most of the time you're having your first dates in America, so just have the tap water. If you happen to love Evian, then order it on a night when you're taking him out.

Conversation

When it comes to chitchat, many women don't realize that their behavior *during* the conversation is just as important as the topic they choose.

"Make an effort to be polite. Just showing up is not good enough. Yes/no answers do not constitute having a conversation."

—Matt, Los Angeles, CA

So, with that in mind, I present:

Janis's Quickest Ways to Ruin Your Date with Conversation

♥ Talk on your cell phone. I warned you about this when you met him and I'm warning you again now! Don't check to see if you have a new message. Don't try to find out who called you earlier. Don't text message. And for the love of God, don't answer your cell phone if it happens to ring! The best place for your cell phone is in your bag, with the power off.

♥ Complain. Don't complain about your roommate, your mother, your car, the weather—anything! Your date is an adult. He understands that everyone's life is full of good things and bad things. Tonight he wants to hear about the good things. Now, I'm not saying you should spend the night bragging about how great you are. Avoid lines like, "My boss just told me how great I was and all my friends agree!" For the first date, you want to walk down the middle of the road. Don't talk about the worst things in your life and don't be so cheerful that it's self-centered.

♥ Check your makeup at the table. As far as your date is concerned, you look beautiful . . . until you start fussing about it. If you must freshen up, go to the restroom, but not every five minutes. And remember what I said before: There's no need to go over the top. Don't return from the bathroom looking like a completely different person from when you left!

> *"Do not check your makeup at the table. We know you don't wake up like that, but reminding us at the table after coffee does not help you. Let the illusion last a little longer."*
>
> —Brian, Chicago, IL

♥ Freak out if he teases you about something. There's a big difference between cruelty and a joke. If you tell a funny story about getting lost on a vacation, he may kid you later about your sense of direction. Roll with it. The fact that he feels comfortable enough to make a little joke around you is a good sign.

> *"Do not overreact to teasing. One of worst things, regardless of beauty, is poor self-esteem. This is a killer."*
>
> —Steven, Houston, TX

♥ Have bad table manners. This is the basic stuff that should be true whenever you go out to eat. But, of course, it's highlighted even more on a date. Cover your mouth when you yawn. Don't chew gum. And, please, whatever you do, don't talk with food in your mouth. It's beyond gross.

♥ Ignore him. Let's assume your date has been nice enough to give you the comfortable seat on the banquette that looks out on all the beautiful people at the restaurant. So don't then spend the evening checking out all those people that you're NOT eating with (even if one of them is Matthew McConaughey). Look at your date. Note: George Clooney is the only exception to this rule because, like you, men think he's the coolest person in the world.

Now that we've covered the basics of how to have a conversation, let's talk about the topics themselves—or, rather, let's talk about topics to avoid!

There are three big areas that are off limits on date number one:

1. Do not talk about marriage and having kids. There's simply no way to talk about this subject without seeming desperate. Most women tell me that they like to bring the subject up, just so the guy knows that she wants to get married and have kids at some point.

Well, guess what? A guy *already assumes* that you're interested in getting married and having kids at some point because you're a woman. But when you talk about this subject on a first date, he'll feel like you don't really care who your husband is, as long as you get one . . . soon! Obviously, this isn't true, so there's no need to give him the wrong impression. There will be lots of time to discuss this in the future. But for now, why don't you get to know each other a bit better?

> *"Don't ask personal, probing questions on a first date. Try to talk about something other than work and how many children a man has or wants. There's plenty of time for that if you like each other."*
>
> —Lou, Los Angeles, CA

2. Do not ask him how much he makes. You can ask him what he does, but don't spend the whole night on this subject. Just like you, he talks about work all day and will be excited to move on to other topics now that it's after quitting time. And he certainly doesn't want to feel like he's in a job interview.

Whatever you do, though, *don't ask him how much he makes.* It's tacky, rude, and, frankly, none of your business at this point. No matter what your intentions, he'll assume you're after the wrong thing (and if you're asking, you probably are).

3. Do not talk about your exes. Ladies, I kid you not, I think every client I surveyed put this topic on their list of dating don'ts. Here's a sampling of some of the comments I got:

♥ "Don't tell me that they are upset because they got dumped last month."
♥ "Don't talk about previous lovers/boyfriends on the first few dates [and] don't mention their money or assets or homes.
♥ "Don't ask questions about a prior relationship too early on (no good can come of it)."

If you talk about how terrible your ex-boyfriend was, your date will wonder why you were ever with that guy in the first place. If you talk about how great he was, your date will wonder why you're not still with that guy. You see where I'm going with this? No matter what you say about your ex-boyfriend, it will be awkward.

And, for the record, men don't like to be grilled about their former flames. Yes, his dating history is a relevant piece of information. But it's much less relevant at the moment than developing a connection between him and you. And talking about former girlfriends is never going to make that happen.

If your date happens to ask you about an ex-boyfriend (unlikely, but it may happen), don't avoid the question, but don't linger on the subject forever. Say a couple of diplomatic sentences and then move on.

Remember, ladies: You're on a date! This is supposed to be fun! I know that getting ready can be a pain in the neck, but now that you've got a glass of wine in you, the tone should be festive.

> *"Do not take the date too seriously. Staying loose will help prevent one of worst cardinal sins: NO FUN!"*
>
> —Brian, Chicago, IL

So what's a safe and upbeat conversation topic? Here are some ideas:

Topic	Janis Says You Can Discuss	But Be Sure the Conversation Doesn't Become
Movies	*The Godfather* (yes, it's true: he's seen it, he loves it) and/or any movie nominated for an Oscar that year	An angry debate about Michael Moore documentaries
Travel	A place you've been and would love to go back to (and why)	A recap of the time you went to Cancún in college and did lots of stuff you now regret

Topic	Janis Says You Can Discuss	But Be Sure the Conversation Doesn't Become
Books	A book you'd think he would like but may not know about	An obscure book that of course he hasn't read but you think makes you sound smart
Your life ambitions	Whether your current job has long-term appeal	A therapy session about what your life ambitions should be

Above all, remember to be a good listener *and* a good talker. There's an old saying that the person who talks the *least* at a social event is usually the one remembered in the best light. It's good to keep that in mind, but it's just as dangerous to have him think you're a mute! If you can maintain a give-and-take style throughout the night, I promise things will go very, very well.

> *"Answer his questions, but always ask your own—not cross-examination questions, but open-ended questions that are at the same intimacy level as his questions."*
> —Adam, New York, NY

Something Sweet

I need to say a quick word about dessert. When I give my dating lectures, women are always wondering if ordering dessert is a good idea. They'll ask me questions like:

♥ Does it make me look fat?
♥ Am I running up the dinner bill?
♥ Does it suggest I didn't like my entrée and I'm still hungry?

The answers are no, no, and no. *Order dessert*. First of all, it goes back to the idea I talked about earlier that men want to see you eat. Yes, he doesn't want you to be obese. But he doesn't want you to be anorexic either. A woman who likes chocolate is normal.

Another reason to order dessert is that it shows the guy you're having a good time. You're not looking to get the check and rush home. You're enjoying his company, so why not keep the date going a bit longer?

But the biggest reason to get dessert is because then your date can have some too. Men love dessert. Any guy who doesn't like brownies is probably an alien.

If you're up for it, you can offer to split a dessert—and, no, the reason for doing this isn't because it makes you look less hungry and less fat. Instead, sharing a dessert is a subtle but romantic gesture. If he doesn't want to share dessert, it isn't because he doesn't want to be intimate with you. It's because he's hungry and wants the chocolate cake all to himself! The good news: You get to have your own piece as well.

The Bill Arrives

When the meal concludes, many women think the following:

Even though he's probably going to pay, I should at least make the effort to split it with him.

Incorrect. Not only does he want to pay, but it's awkward for you to make this half-hearted attempt to split the bill. When someone offers to do something nice for you—in this case, he has offered to take you out to dinner—let them. If your friend picks you up at the airport, it's rude if you suddenly offer them cash. Same idea applies here. Just thank him for treating you to dinner and you'll be all set.

Many women assume that there are a boatload of exceptions to this "let him pay" rule, but this conventional wisdom is almost always wrong. Here's what I mean:

Confusing situation:	You should pay if you have no intention of hooking up with him.
Janis says:	He'll respect you more if you *don't* sleep with him just because he bought you dinner. Your date isn't twelve years old. He doesn't expect sex as a payment for every nice gesture he makes. Remember: You're his date, not his Madame.
Confusing situation:	You recommended the restaurant and it winds up being much more expensive than you thought it would be.
Janis says:	If he asks for your recommendation, he's prepared to go anywhere. If he has a budget, he'll do a little bit of research to be sure that he doesn't find himself in an embarrassing situation.

Confusing situation:	You should pay if you clearly make more money than he does—like if you're an investment banker and he's a high school history teacher.
Janis says:	Offering to pay in this situation only makes it seem like the difference in your salaries is a big problem for you (or that you think it should be a big problem for him). He wouldn't have asked you out to dinner if he couldn't afford it. Under those circumstances, your offer to pay is condescending and a HUGE blow to his ego.
Confusing situation:	The bill arrives while he's in the bathroom.
Janis says:	Most men won't go to the bathroom when the bill is about to arrive to avoid this very scenario. But if it happens, just put the bill in the center of the table and wait for him to return.

If it's important to you that you contribute financially on the first date, you can always pick up a smaller expense, such as the cab ride home at the end of the night. Or, if you don't have dessert at the restaurant, you can take him out for ice cream.

But no matter how many dates you guys go on, I think you should avoid splitting the bill. Guys find it way more romantic for the two of you to take each other out. And if one meal winds up being more expensive than another, that's okay. Don't try to keep track of every nickel and dime you're each spending. It suddenly feels like you're dating your accountant.

Until We Meet Again...

As the night winds down, most women nervously assume that there is some written set of "man rules" that says how much love a guy should be given at the end of the first date depending on what transpired that evening:

> *He took me to the nicest sushi restaurant in town, so he's at least expecting that I'll make out with him, right?*

No! Let's go through this again: Your date will respect you more if you don't equate sex with money. He'll want any intimacy that comes his way to be a result of your attraction to him, not the tab for the evening.

In reality, all a guy wants from you after a first date is a sign. If you want to go out again, make sure he knows it. No guy ever wants to call a woman for a second date and be shot down; it's way too demoralizing. So he wants to know by the end of the first date what your answer would be if he calls again.

How do you let him know what you're thinking? There are three great ways to communicate that you want to see him again:

1. Kiss him on the lips. This doesn't need to be a high school tongue-fest. A warm, deliberate kiss that lasts a few seconds longer than it needs to will do the trick. It's a great way for you to communicate your feelings without using words.

"Being honest about how you feel is sexy to me. A nice kiss at the end of the night means a lot. To forgo that is kind of a turn-off."

—Will, Boston, MA

2. Verbally schedule another date. Nothing sends a message more clearly than saying, "This was a lot of fun. I'd love to see you again soon." Don't worry—you won't sound desperate. Instead, he'll perceive you as a confident woman who knows what she wants to do (and that's *very* attractive).

3. Send him an e-mail (or call) the next day saying you had a great time and would love to go out again. ALWAYS do this!

STORY TIME

Let me tell you a story about sending a thank-you e-mail after a date. I have a client named Henry whom I set up with five different women, of which he really liked four. But the one girl he wasn't crazy about, Vanessa, sent him a very sweet e-mail the day after the date and thanked Henry for a wonderful evening. Henry was so impressed with Vanessa's thoughtfulness that *she* was the one he went out with again (and again, and again).

Okay, I actually have another story about thank-you e-mails because they're so friggin' important. One of my clients, Orlando, goes out on a date with a woman named Maya. They were both psyched for the date, but afterward, Orlando gave the evening a B– He liked Maya, but she just seemed a little off her game and he wasn't sure if it was going to work.

But then he got an e-mail from Maya saying she knew she was off her game but she really wanted to go out again and hoped Orlando wanted to as well. It turns out that Maya had to take a business trip earlier in the week and she just was run down by the time the date arrived. She didn't want to cancel, though, because she was excited about the date. And she didn't want to talk about her business trip and explain why she was tired, because that just seemed lame. So the thank-you note gave her an opportunity to explain the details of her situation, as well as telling Orlando that she wanted to go out again . . . which is exactly what happened.

Bottom line: Whatever you do, you've got to let him know what you're thinking.

Warning!

What you are *not obligated* to do after the first date is invite him in. This opens up a lot of complications. You have to worry about your roommates, your cats, and the piles of stuff strewn about your place from when you were getting ready. It's good to have the boundaries of your life and space crossed gradually. It extends the mystery and helps you avoid going too far before you really know who you're with. A person can tell a lot—and may jump to the wrong conclusions—by the things a person owns.

Plus, once he's there, there's the issue of getting him to leave. You don't want to go too far on the first date. You'll seem too easy—a big turnoff for guys—and you'll be rushing through the courtship.

If there's a sexual connection between the two of you, you should let it build slowly, like the plot of a movie. If a cop catches the bad guy five minutes into the film, the next hour and half gets really boring. Same can be true of relationships. Let the sexual tension build over the course of several dates and it will be much more satisfying to both of you when you finally act on it.

Now, I know there are exceptions to this rule. If your place is immaculate (and empty), the night is still young, and you've both had such a great time that you don't want it to end, then there is a right way to do a nightcap. The trick is to *pace yourself*. You can drink for a bit, talk for a bit, and kiss for a bit, but you should still save some excitement for future dates. So after a while, say you're getting sleepy and escort him to the door. If he doesn't take the hint, you can tell him you want to save some more fun for next time. That will leave him feeling good and looking forward to the next date.

By the way, don't be a tease when you say goodnight. It drives men crazy. If you're sprawled out on the couch kissing, it's a little awkward to suddenly stand up and say you're tired. So don't let things go too far before cutting him off. And if you really want to play it safe, save your kissing for after you've walked him to the door.

Thanks, but No Thanks

The hardest part about any first date is trying to figure out whether the guy wants to see you again. The problem is that almost all guys tell you they had a nice time and will call you soon. But sometimes, that's a load of crap. They may have had a nice time, but then they never call again. It's beyond frustrating, isn't it?

Look, I wish I had some magic answer here. I wish I could say that if a guy asks you up to his place at the end of the night, he definitely wants to see you again. Or if the guy gives you a long kiss goodnight, he's already falling for you. But the thing is, those rules don't always hold up. The only time you can be certain he wants to see you again is when he calls.

It sucks, I know. I mean it's one of the hardest and most unfair parts of dating. Why don't men have the balls to just tell us yes or no at the end of the night so we're not wandering around in limbo? Men hate confrontation with women. They'll argue with each other until they're blue in the face, but when it comes to their dating life, they'd rather sneak away than tell you how they really feel.

The best thing you can do is to make sure he knows how you feel and not read too much into his signs . . . because he probably doesn't know he's giving you signs. Whatever he says, whatever he does—the only way you know he wants to go out again is when he calls. I wish that wasn't the reality, but, well, it is.

There's one more first date question that's really important to talk about:

How do I end the date if I DON'T want to see him again?

For the record, ladies, I almost always recommend giving a guy another chance. In my book, a guy gets three strikes before he is out. There are lots of reasons why people could be off their game—stress from work, illness, family member driving them crazy. So, if you're up for it, give him another chance—you'd want him to do the same for you.

But I'm realistic.

STORY TIME

I had a client, Mark, whom I set up with a woman named Angela. I had a great feeling about this match. I mean, Angela was everything Mark had been looking for. It was perfect. It couldn't fail. But it did—and not because Angela did anything wrong. She was fabulous. She was exactly as advertised. And all Mark could tell me was, "Janis, on paper this woman was everything I wanted—she was smart, she was funny, she looked like Sandra Bullock—but for some reason there wasn't a spark. Everything was just too bland and vanilla."

I get it. It's disappointing, but it happens. There are times when you'll feel that way too. So if you do decide that you're definitely not interested, you need to communicate that to your date at the end of the night. Here's how:

Thank him politely. Don't slam the door in his face just because he's not your future husband.

Give him a quick kiss on the cheek. Lips = want to see you again. Cheek = thanks a lot and best wishes.

Don't be confusing. You've politely thanked him. It's time for the date to end. Don't talk until the wee hours of the morning. Don't kiss him several times. Don't give him the phone number of the hotel you'll be at on an upcoming business trip. All of those things will send mixed signals and confuse the guy. Just close the door and end the date.

You don't have to tell him directly that you don't want to go out again . . . unless he asks you point blank. Frankly, you should welcome such bluntness because it gives you the chance to avoid any future confusion. Whatever you do, though, don't get nervous and lie.

Don't say you want to go out with him again if you don't! Trust me: He can take it. He's heard it before. If he couldn't handle you saying it, he shouldn't have asked the question in the first place.

With that in mind, here's a related issue that everyone finds confusing:

Do you call to say thank you for a date (that he paid for) if you don't want to see him again?

Here's what I think: You don't have to call him if you don't want to see him again. No matter what you say, he'll think you're calling because you want to go out again. Seriously. You can even say, "Thank you so much, but I don't want to go out again," and he'll think, well, she called, so she's clearly into me!

However, e-mail is a great option here. I already said that sending an e-mail was a good idea if you want to see him again, but it also works well if you *don't* want to go out again. So go ahead and send him an e-mail the next day thanking him again for dinner and wishing him good luck in the future. I really recommend doing this: It's simple, effective, and very classy.

The Sexy Chart!

I want to take a second to summarize some of the important advice I've given you in this chapter. I know that I've done this in the two previous chapters, but this chart is the most important of the three. Why? Because experience has shown me that the first date is where a lot of women REALLY mess up. I'm not talking about dates that go bad because the guy and the girl are a terrible match. I'm talking about dates that are a disaster because the woman is CLUELESS!

So I'll repeat myself three thousand times if I have to. I want you to find a great man, and in order to do that, you have to realize what is sexy on a first date:

What's Sexy on a First Date

♥ Wearing a skirt . . . not pants!

♥ Getting your hair blown out. No ponytails!

♥ Looking like you didn't just come from work.

♥ Letting him kiss you hello on the cheek.

♥ Having a drink with him (but not three or four).

♥ Eating and enjoying your dinner and dessert (food is sexy!).

♥ Having fun when you talk to him. It's a date, not a eulogy!

♥ Letting him kiss you goodnight on the lips.

♥ Sending him a thank-you e-mail.

And, of course, there's also the other side of things:

What's NOT Sexy on a First Date

👎 Dressing slutty and showing too much cleavage.

👎 Being late.

👎 Talking on your cell phone at any point during the date.

👎 Checking your makeup at the table.

👎 Being indecisive when you order.

👎 Being rude to the waiter . . . or anyone else.

👎 Getting drunk.

👎 Asking him about ex-girlfriends.

👎 Asking him how much he makes.

👎 Asking him about whether he wants children.

👎 Sleeping with him at the end of the night.

Not What You're After

You need to be careful of guys who won't acknowledge that they're actually on a date with you. The most obvious warning sign is when a guy simply refuses to use the word *date*, and instead refers to the evening as "going out," or a "dinner with someone new." It's a date. And if he can't commit to a first date, imagine how he'll feel about calling you his girlfriend!

Even if he calls the evening of the date, there are other warning signs to be on the lookout for, such as:

♥ He's given no thought to planning the evening.
♥ He's invited other friends along to join you (and talks mostly to them).
♥ He says, "You look so hot tonight" one too many times.

Sometimes a man will get creative and give you a line like, "I just don't believe in labels." Or, "I don't like doing things the way society tells me to." Those lines are garbage. It's great for a guy to be original. But he also has to acknowledge the truth about what's happening—namely, you're on a date! If he can't do that, he's trouble.

Let Him Down Easy

Sometimes you think you're being very obvious in telling a guy that you don't want to go out again but, for some reason, he just doesn't take the hint. You don't give him a kiss good-night; you don't let him walk you home; you tell him you'll be out of town on business for the next month . . . and yet he still calls you the next day to ask when you can go out again.

In that case, you must do the right thing: *Call him back.* One of the biggest complaints I get from guys is that they absolutely hate it when women never return a phone call or an e-mail. It's rude. So even if he's not the one for you, call him back.

Yes, it's difficult, but it's much classier than never calling him back or—even worse—going out with him again because you don't feel like telling him the truth.

He'll be upset, but he'll live to fight another day. And so will you.

Part Two

I Think We're Dating

CHAPTER 5

Do We Still Have Stuff to Talk About?

The Second, Third, and Subsequent Dates

What's the big difference between the first date and the second date? I always tell my clients that it comes down to nerves.

On the first date, everyone is nervous—the guy, the girl, and even me, if I've set the couple up! And when you're nervous, strange stuff happens. It's Murphy's Law—whatever can go wrong on a first date usually does.

Here are just some of the first-date mishaps that my clients have experienced over the years:

- ♥ Spilled food all over themselves (and their date).
- ♥ Sprayed water all over their pants while washing their hands in the bathroom and returned to the table with a big, wet spot on their crotch.
- ♥ Got lost getting to the restaurant (even if they were the one who picked the place!).
- ♥ Sweated so much that their shirt turned a darker shade of blue.
- ♥ Horribly mispronounced a French word while trying to order wine.
- ♥ Told the same story twice (or three times).
- ♥ Called the date by the wrong name (that was a HUGE mistake!).

Many times, a first date doesn't lead to a second date. There's an X-factor in matchmaking that you simply can't account for until two people actually spend an evening together. Since there's so much that can go wrong on a first date (even with my help!) everyone has their share of one-and-done relationships.

So if it turns out that you both want to see each other again, you should be really excited. You're both going to be a lot less nervous the second time around. You're already familiar with each other, and that takes away a ton of pressure. Plus, you already know that the other person is interested in you. If they weren't, they wouldn't be going out with you again!

The Planning, Part 2

Okay, so there's a spark between the two of you and now we get to fan the flames and build a fire.

The question at the top of every woman's list when it comes to the second date is:

If he planned the first date, am I supposed to plan the second date?

Let me tell you: Men are thrilled to have you take some initiative and plan the second date. It shows that you're really excited about going out again, which is music to his ears.

> "Do not make the man make every decision. We really want a strong partner type, and a woman who knows what she wants is a big plus."
>
> —Steven, Houston, TX

So here are the steps you should take to make sure the planning of the second date goes smoothly:

Step #1: Wait for Him to Call

Guys may like the idea of you planning date number two, but they still like to take the lead on scheduling the date. Even if you called to set up the first date (which was bold and awesome of you), men still like to have the ball in their court this time around.

If you haven't heard from him, you can drop him an e-mail just to check in. That way, there's no doubt about your feelings and he knows he has the green light to call you for date number two. Just be sure you use spell-check!

If he still doesn't call, it's because he doesn't want to go out again. Let me repeat that because it's VERY important.

> IF HE DOESN'T CALL TO SCHEDULE A SECOND DATE, IT'S BECAUSE HE DOESN'T WANT TO GO OUT AGAIN.

If you kissed him at the end of the first date and e-mailed him that you had a good time and want to go out again, he has all the data he needs. He's not nervous or confused. He didn't lose your number. He didn't get called away to Zimbabwe on business for a month. There's radio silence because he doesn't want to go out again. And if that's the case, it's time to move on. You don't want to date a guy who doesn't want to be with you. End of story.

Step #2: Have Ideas Ready for When He Does Call

Once he does call, the ball is now in your court. Now, guys *don't* want you to come across as General George Patton, barking out commands for where and when he should meet you. That's a little scary.

Instead, have a couple of ideas that you're excited about and pitch them to him. I promise—he'll be thrilled to hear your ideas and will gladly follow your lead. If you need to, it's okay to write down your ideas ahead of time to avoid an embarrassing mind blank.

Try to come up with a plan that differs from what you did on date one. In all likelihood, you had drinks and/or dinner the first time you went out. Lovely. But there's no need to have the exact same date all over again. There are lots of different options you can suggest:

Good Alternatives to Having Dinner at a Restaurant for Date Number Two

♥ Brunch
♥ Museums
♥ Movies
♥ Live entertainment (concert, theater, sports)
♥ Something sporty (biking, sailing, etc.)

Needless to say, not every activity will be right for the two of you—if he gets seasick, then maybe sailing isn't the best idea. But every guy will be ready to do something besides dinner . . . especially if you're excited about it as well.

Step #3: Be Prepared for the Possibility That He May Have Planned Something Already

When a guy calls to schedule date number two, there's a good chance he has already made plans. Maybe he got a dinner reservation at a hard-to-get-into restaurant. Maybe he remembered that you said you like baseball and someone just offered him tickets to Friday night's game.

Under those circumstances, it's okay for you to go with his plans again if you want to. If he's already planned the second date it means he's *really* into you—he wouldn't have made the effort if he wasn't.

Mixing It Up

The first date was about the two of you getting to know each other.

The second date is about figuring out if you two can really date each other and have a relationship. It's not enough to relive the first date again and again. There has to be growth. Men want to know if the two of you will find each other interesting for a prolonged period of time. Here's what that translates into for the second date:

♥ New conversation topics. Let's say that on the first date the two of you talked about travel—where you've been, where you want to go, and how you want to get there. It was good stuff. But that date's over, and you need to spend the next date talking about different topics. So show up with some new interests you want to discuss.

♥ Attraction. I'm not talking about sex (yet). Right now, I'm just talking about a vibe and a comfort level between the two of you. If he puts his arm around you, it's got to feel good. When you kiss him at the end of a date, it should be comfortable and exciting. You've got to show him with your body language that it's okay for him to get closer to you—emotionally and physically. If you don't, he's going to quickly lose interest.

> "I hate it when I get the feeling the woman is not physically connected or simply doesn't like sex that much."
>
> —Roger, Baltimore, MD

♥ Honesty. When you guys were first meeting each other, I talked about the importance of being honest about who you are—don't tell him you were an Olympic swimmer if you weren't. Now it's time to start being honest about how you feel toward him.

How many times have you been out with a guy who you thought was really into you, only to have him suddenly call things off. It sucks, right? Well, believe it or not, the out-of-blue-breakup happens to guys too, and it sucks just as much for them as it did for you. So if you're not feeling good about things, don't pretend you are. And, on the flip side, if you are into him, there's no need to play it cool and pretend you hate him.

> "Any appearance of playing hard to get is just a big turnoff and seems disingenuous."
>
> —Will, Boston, MA

Let me talk about playing hard to get for a moment. A lot of women tell me:

Janis, I've found who the men who chase me the most are the ones I don't actually want. Some men seem to take rejection as a challenge!

That's absolutely right. But this goes right back to what I said in Chapter Three. This is such a common mistake that women make that I want to repeat what I've already said:

> MEN LIKE A LITTLE CHALLENGE, BUT THEY DON'T LIKE MANIPULATION AND GAMES!

Remember my warning about *The Rules*! At this point in the relationship, playing hard to get is a game. You're already on your second date and things are moving along nicely. If you slam on the brakes or suddenly become hard to reach, it isn't a challenge . . . it's just strange. And mature guys won't put up with it for very long.

Now, should you play hard to get when you're first meeting someone? I really don't think you need to. If a guy is still obsessed with chasing after things he can't have, then I seriously doubt he's ready to settle down with anyone. You don't need to stalk him, but you should never be afraid to tell a guy how you feel. If he'd rather go off and chase some woman who's not available, then screw him.

STORY TIME

I have a client named Lance who's thirty-eight and divorced. I set him up with a woman named Anne. They went out *seven times* and Anne never once asked where the relationship was going. Eventually I told Anne she was crazy. I mean, Lance was my client, but I totally had to take Anne's side here. I told her, "Sweetie, you're forty-one years old, you've been out on SEVEN dates with this guy. You've got to push the envelope. Instead of worrying whether you should see each other on Thursday or Monday, you should suggest seeing each other on both Thursday and Monday."

So guess what happened? Well, it wasn't a fairy tale ending. Anne did push the envelope, and then she and Lance broke up. Now a lot of women will say:

See Janis? You show interest in a guy and he pushes you away!

But let's not take our eyes off the prize here. What did Anne learn? She learned that Lance wasn't the right guy for her, and that was a pretty important piece of information. She didn't waste more time with him, and I quickly set her up with another client. So, in a way, it was a fairy tale ending because she didn't marry the guy who didn't want to be with her.

Look, the only way you are ever going to figure out if someone is the right person for you is by *spending time with them*. You shouldn't have to beg for the man of your dreams to go out with you. He should want to spend time with you so you can discover whether or not the relationship is meant to be.

And you definitely shouldn't be with a guy who gets turned on when you ignore him. It may lead to some kinky sex, but the long-term health of that relationship is doomed.

Intimacy

At the end of the second date, you're once again faced with the decision of how sexually intimate you want to be with the guy. I tell woman that there are two rules for the end of the second date:

Rule #1

Whatever you did at the end of the first date, the guy is expecting at least that much at the end of the second date. That's why it was really important that you didn't go too far after date number one.

Rule #2

DON'T SLEEP WITH HIM YET!

It's perfectly fine for you to play it safe and not invite him up to your place at the end of the second date. As with the first date, you're probably putting yourself in a situation that's going to end awkwardly. He may think you're inviting him up for sex, and when it's clear that you're not, things can get uncomfortable.

If you had dinner by his place and he invites *you* up, you have two choices. If you feel comfortable, then you can say yes and head up to his place for a while. Just because you're going up to his place, though, doesn't mean you have to have sex with him and/or spend the night. (Have I said that enough? Well, it's true!)

Have a drink, talk for a bit, and if the moment seems right, slide up next to him on the couch and kiss for a while. I wouldn't go much further than that because then it becomes difficult to find the right place to put on the brakes.

If you're not comfortable going up to his place yet, DON'T GO! I don't want you putting yourself in a difficult situation . . . and that's exactly what it will be if you're uncomfortable with the idea. Just politely decline the offer, give him a kiss, and tell him you're excited to go out again.

Now, obviously, if you're NEVER comfortable with the idea of going up to his place, he's not the right man for you. Sooner or later you're going to have to be alone with him in the bedroom or break things off. But after the second date, it's still okay to send the message that you need a little more time. And if he freaks out . . . well, that's his problem.

The bottom line is that you just need to keep things moving in the right direction. Your date should get the feeling that you're moving toward more intimacy, not away from it. So if you kissed him at the end of the first date, then the kiss at the end of this date should be longer and more passionate . . . but that's all for now.

If you invited him up at the end of the first date, you're pretty much obliged to do it again. You can't make out on the couch at the end of the first date and then shake his hand at the end of the second date. If you do that, there won't be a third date. So pace yourself. If you go too fast too soon, you won't have anything left for future dates.

Phone a Friend

By the time the second date ends, you're both officially free from the dilemma of "can I call him or does he want to call me?" In my book, once you've made it through two dates, you can call each other whenever you want—including the scheduling of a third date.

Here are just a few words of advice that my clients want me to pass on about when you call him to plan date number three:

- ♥ Don't leave phone messages that ramble on for several minutes. You can be cute while still being brief.
- ♥ You don't have to awkwardly reintroduce yourself at the beginning of the call. He knows who you are!

♥ If you leave him a message, give him time to return the call. If he's at a doctor's appointment for an hour, he doesn't need six messages from you on his cell when he's done.

♥ You don't need to leave the same message at his home, job, and on his cell phone. He checks them all throughout the day.

♥ When you do talk on the phone, try to talk to *him*—not to your friend who's in the room with you or to your dog that just did something hilarious.

♥ Phone sex voice is not necessary. He prefers actual sex.

More than anything, just be *relaxed* when you call. Don't hyperventilate while you're on the phone with him. Remember: There's no reason to be nervous. At this point, he's into you, and he'll be thrilled to get your call.

Third Time's the Charm

By the third date, the guy is now looking for more than just some fun conversation topics and a long kiss goodnight. The emotional bond needs to be strong. Date three is when the two of you turn the corner. After three good dates, you're an item. Which means it's really important to understand what separates the third date from the second date:

♥ Daytime Encounters. Sooner or later, a guy will want to see you at other times of the day besides Thursday night. People's lives don't exist solely between 7 p.m. and 1 a.m. If you're going to be part of his life and vice versa, you need to start seeing each other during the day.

♥ Trust. You don't need to hand over your social security number and mother's maiden name just because you're going out again. But it's nice if you feel like you can begin to tell him more personal things about your life. If you have a medical issue that you're dealing with, for example, that's going to have to come up in conversation sooner or later. The first or second date is too early— why have a hard conversation if you're not even sure you want to date this guy yet?

But when you're ready to make the leap from "going on a couple of dates" to "relationship," you have to feel like you can tell the guy all about yourself. And, obviously, you need to have these conversations *before you guys start sleeping together*. Healthy relations have trust before sex.

If you don't feel comfortable talking about personal stuff after several dates, it's probably a sign that this guy isn't your soul mate. On the flip side, if you feel like you can open up, he'll feel like he can do the same, and that's how a solid bond is formed.

And if you wind up telling him something personal and it causes him to freak out and break up with you, then it's clear he didn't really want to be dating you in the first place.

STORY TIME

I'm going to borrow a story from my personal life. Actually, it's from my *daughter's* personal life (it's not easy having a mom who's a matchmaker, is it, sweetheart?). Anyway, she's been dating this guy for a while. One night he comes over to take my daughter out and she's still upstairs getting ready. So he has to sit and talk to me (lucky guy!). And, because I'm me, I have to ask him about dating. So, point blank, I say, "Why do you love my daughter?" (Can you believe I did this to the poor guy?!) And the boyfriend looks at me and says, "I feel comfortable around her." It was a good answer. It was short, it was simple, but it said so much. And then, mercifully, my daughter came downstairs and rescued her boyfriend from my interview!

But keep those words in mind: Comfort leads to love. If you don't have one, you're not going to have the other.

♥ Satisfaction. Remember my client Jay from the last chapter? The guy who hates it when women order bottled water on a first date? Well, he also made a very interesting point about what he thinks relationships are all about:

> *"At the end of the day, it all comes down to this: Can I make you happy?"*
>
> —Jay, Los Angeles, CA

It's a really smart observation. For men, there's a great satisfaction in making you happy. If they feel like they can't do that, the relationship is never going to work. And if you're the sort of person who's just never happy, that's not going to work either.

♥ Priority. If you've been out on a couple of dates, men want to feel like they are becoming an important part of your life. They want you to return their e-mails the same day they're sent; they want you to make time to see them even if your social schedule is busy; they want you to answer your cell phone when they call it. Is that asking a lot? Sure it is. But you better be asking the same of him!

♥ Exclusivity. You don't need to be a neurosurgeon to figure out this one, ladies. If he's going on multiple dates with you, he's into you. And if he's into you, he doesn't want you to be seeing anyone else. So if you're kinda-sorta-maybe-partly dating some other guy, it's time to break it off NOW!

♥ The (Annoying) Details. On the first few dates, you and the guy were on your best behavior. But the more time you spend together the more your imperfections and odd habits are going to show up.

The third date is the time to start thinking about the big picture. Are you guys really compatible for the long term? You have to decide whether each of your personal traits—one of you bites your nails while the other one is an obsessive list maker—are deal-breakers or things you can live with.

The third date also marks the moment where you should start to pay for *some* of the date. I don't want you paying for dinner. It's still too early in the relationship for that. And if he's insisting you pay, then watch out. He may not be a keeper after all.

I usually tell my clients that date number three should be an activity such as going to the movies or a ballgame. This gives you the perfect opportunity to contribute without breaking the bank. If he gets the tickets, you get the soda and popcorn. If you go to a baseball game, you can get the hot dogs and beer.

> *"If he takes you out to dinner and a movie, buying the popcorn is a small but VERY nice and VERY appreciated gesture. Do it. He will tell his mom that you did and she will like you forever."*
>
> —Dave, New York, NY

Now, *how* you offer to pay is very important. Here are a few things to keep in mind when you offer to pick up part of the snacks:

♥ Be sincere. Don't be half-hearted when you offer to get the popcorn at the movies. You know what I mean, ladies. You softly say, "It's on me" as you reach for your bag in super-slow motion. If you're going to make the gesture, then be glad to do it. Otherwise, the whole thing is meaningless.

♥ Don't make an overly big deal about it. Don't make little comments like, "Popcorn is so expensive" or "Five bucks for a hot dog—what a rip off!" That only makes your date feel awkward about letting you buy the snacks. If you make money a big deal, it will be. Instead, make the personal connection between the two of you the focal point of the evening—not how expensive everything is.

♥ He might insist on paying. You want to avoid a battle over who's paying. If he adamantly insists on getting everything, it's okay to let him pay. Your (heartfelt!) gesture was all he needed.

If you want to do more than just buy popcorn, you can always get him a little gift that ties into the conversations the two of you have been having. For example, I have a client named Rick who went on three dates with a woman named Brooke. Rick insisted on paying for all the dates (which, of course, I loved). Brooke was also impressed, and so she wanted to do something nice in return. They had been talking a lot about classical music, and so Brooke went out and got Rick a CD of a Mozart piano concerto that had come up in conversation. Suffice to say, Rick was thrilled. He liked the CD, but he LOVED the gesture. That $14 CD was worth so much more than a $75 dinner because it was something very personal that the two of them had discussed.

Music, books, a bottle of wine—all of these simple gifts can go a long way if they represent a connection between the two of you.

Now, there's one other third date scenario we haven't talked about yet:

What if I want to cook him dinner?

The third date is a good time to do this. The guy will be flattered that you're making such a nice effort—not to mention how happy he'll be when he tastes your masterpieces! But you need to keep a few things in mind:

1. You'll have to pay. He'll probably offer to bring a bottle of wine or some ice cream, and that's great. But you'll be the one who's dropping $50 on ingredients at the su-

permarket. If you're fine with that expense, then there's no problem. But whatever you do, don't ask him to split the grocery bill with you. Tacky!

2. He'll be in your place. As I've already said, this can be a tricky situation at the end of the evening. But you'll have to deal with it because he's already there for dinner. If you're comfortable with having him over, then that's great. But if you're not, then hold off on cooking him dinner until later in the relationship.

3. Only do it if you can actually cook. If you happen to be a great cook, that's a big plus. Obviously, modern men don't expect that you'll stay home and do all the cooking. But who doesn't want to be married to a skilled chef? Yum! Anyway, if cooking is your thing, then it's fine to show it off. If it isn't, that's okay too, but there's no need to pretend like it is.

Not What You're After

When it comes to scheduling dates, I tell women to give guys the benefit of the doubt for the first date, but not for the second or third date.

I'll explain what I mean by that with an example from my own life.

STORY TIME

Long before I was married, some girlfriends and I went to the Concord Hotel in the Catskill Mountains of New York for a long weekend. While I was there, I met a guy from

Quebec. We talked for a bit, exchanged numbers, and then I never heard from him again.

A *year* later he calls me to ask me out. Seriously! It was a friggin' year later! Unbelievable, right? When I asked him why it took so long to call, he said, "Janis, I told you I'd call you. I just didn't say when." To be honest, I laughed. And we wound up going out a few times.

If a guy takes forever to schedule a first date, I think it's still okay to go out with him if you're up for it. But if he takes forever to schedule dates number two or three, then I'd be concerned. That guy from Quebec took a year to call me for date number one, but after that he called me all the time.

After you've had a first date, the guy needs to pick up the pace. If a week—or several weeks—go by after the first date and then, out of the blue, you get a call from him, *be careful*. I mean, if that isn't a warning sign, I don't know what is! And if he has a legit excuse, it better be good!

If he doesn't have a good excuse, proceed at your own risk! More than likely, he just wants a booty call, and figured you were a good option.

Let Him Down Easy

Earlier in this chapter, I talked about the importance of a sexual attraction growing between the two of you. If you are committing to a second or third date, you should be comfortable with the idea that some level of physical intimacy is going to enter the equation. If you're not feeling attracted to him by this point, you should call things off.

I had a client named Joe who's a very fancy guy. I set him

up with a woman named Wendy, and Wendy loved going out with Joe. He treated her like a goddess, and every date was a wonderful adventure—black-tie events, a cruise on his yacht, fabulous meals . . . you get the idea—it was a fairy tale. One problem: Wendy didn't want to sleep with Joe. The spark just wasn't there. Finally, after TEN dates, she broke it off. And I told her, "Wendy, you're being ridiculous! You knew after three or four dates that the spark wasn't there, but you kept going out with him because he showed you a good time." It was totally unfair to Joe and I was beyond annoyed with Wendy.

Now, I'm NOT saying you have to run off and sleep with each other after date number three. But you should be feeling like you'll want to sleep with him at some point. As you can imagine, if you're not sexually attracted to him but continue to go on dates, the guy is going to develop a bit of a "what's wrong with me?" complex.

You've had enough time. If there's no spark, let someone else have a chance.

CHAPTER 6

I Won't Laugh at Your Underwear If You Don't Laugh at Mine

Your First Night Together

Tell the truth: When you looked at the table of contents for this book, you immediately skipped ahead to this chapter, right? It's okay—I would have done the same thing.

And while we're on the subject of confessions, here's a fact that always shocks women: My male clients LOVE to talk to me about sex. It's true! Needless to say, I'm more than happy to listen and give my advice. But most women think it's kind of surprising that men actually want to analyze their sex life. We ladies tend to think that if men are discussing sex, it's only to brag to their guy friends about who they've slept with (and how quickly).

Men are obsessed with sex (and, let's be honest ladies, aren't you?), but it's one thing to be infatuated and quite another to express your feelings openly . . . to me! In this case, men do both, which means sex is a more complex topic for men than most women think.

Before the Big Night

Let's start our sex-ed class with an obvious question:

How soon into a relationship do guys want to have intercourse? Is it really as soon as the first date? Or is there a certain number of dates after which they either want to have sex or break up?

I've alluded to this in earlier chapters, but now let me say it point blank: Never, ever have sex on the first few dates. Obviously, a lot of guys *would* have sex on a first date, but they don't actually want you to do it.

What?

I sound like a whackadoodle, right? I mean, if men would have sex, then why shouldn't you be just as open to it?

Here's why: You'll seem cheap, easy, and beyond desperate. A guy may go ahead and sleep with you because men don't turn down sex, but he'll have ZERO respect for you. And if he has no respect for you, he won't want to keep dating you.

If a guy is really into you, he wants to let the excitement build. And he wants to see that you don't just sleep with any guy who buys you dinner.

> *"Do not have sex until at least eight to ten dates. It depends on the person, but this oldie is really a goodie. Alpha males respect what is hard to get and tend to keep what is difficult to retain. It's basic but very real."*
>
> —Adam, New York, NY

Or, to put it another way:

> "Don't give it up until after at least a couple of weeks."
> —Matt, Washington, D.C.

Men are totally happy waiting a while before sex. Now, I hear the skeptics among you:

Come on, Janis! Eight to ten dates before intercourse?! That's crazy. If we haven't had sex by date four or five, he's going to be gone!

Look, I'll be honest with you—the range that I hear over and over again from my clients is five to ten dates. The exact number obviously depends on the two of you. In some cases, sleeping together after date number five is appropriate, and in others, date twelve makes more sense.

Also, you want him to connect (if not commit) to you before you sleep with him, otherwise you're skipping a really important step that you can't just go back and make up.

Needless to say, if you wait too long, the guy is going to lose interest. Some guys will wait longer than others to have sex. Since it's hard to give you an exact number between five and ten, my expert advice is to *wait until you feel there's an emotional commitment.* Men will sleep with a woman even if they don't know her name; men will sleep with women while they're seeing other people; men will sleep with women whom they won't ask out on Valentine's Day; men will sleep with women they don't want to see on a Saturday night because they don't want to send a signal that they're getting serious.

But a guy who really loves you and wants to be with you all

the time—including Saturdays and Valentine's Day and the day he usually plays poker—will happily wait to have sex . . . and that's why you should too.

STORY TIME

Here's what I'm talking about: I have a client, Reed, who's a bit of a jet-setter. I set him up with a woman named Liz and she slept with him after the second date. I was shocked, to say the least. So what do you think happened? Well, Reed was flying around the country on business, and every time he was back in New York, he'd ring up Liz for a booty call. Reed didn't go into the relationship looking for a sex buddy, but that's what happened because Liz slept with him too soon. Reed shares some of blame for things not working out, but Liz was the one who wound up not getting what she wanted. Needless to say, Liz eventually broke up with Reed and everyone was back at square one.

Obviously, your boyfriend isn't going to drop the sex topic and never bring it up again . . . after all, men will try their damnest to get what they want! The best thing to do is just be honest and tell him what you're thinking point blank. Tell him he's great, you're loving the relationship, but you're just not ready for sex. In this case, the simplest solution is the best one.

The good news is that most of the time this conversation will take place on its own. In the modern world of STDs, guys aren't just hopping in the sack with someone without being safe and smart about it.

Needless to say, I support the safety first approach to modern love. And so when you're having that conversation about who's been tested for what and how recently, it's a great moment to talk about whether or not you're ready for sex.

Remember: You can't take forever, but you can take as long as you need to feel comfortable. And if you're not feeling comfortable after ten dates, what does that tell you?

Preparations

Once the two of you have been together long enough that the time seems right, there are also a couple of things men want you to take care of before you two enter the bedroom. (And, no, it doesn't involve buying a French maid's outfit . . . usually.)

Here are some advance-planning tips that will keep things running smoothly on the big night:

♥ Be decisive. This is the most important issue to men. You NEVER, ever have to have sex with a guy if you don't want to. But men want you to make up your mind before you're in bed together. Of course, you have the right to say no at any point in time and you *never surrender that right*. But from a guy's point of view, if you're willing to take off your clothes, hopefully your mind is already made up. If you hem and haw while he's standing there naked, it's a big turn-off.

♥ Be clean. Don't worry about the stuff you can't control—a birthmark, a scar, and so on. Instead, work on the stuff you can control—armpit hair, leg hair, dry skin, a rash. And, yes, a little grooming "down there" is a big turn on for guys. You don't have to get the Brazilian (although he'll love it), but you do have to show him that you're not still living in the 1970s—know what I mean?

♥ Be up front. If you have a tattoo/piercing/other-body-art that's a little unusual, some guys will get turned on by your wild side. However, a little heads-up beforehand isn't the worst idea, just so he doesn't get scared by the large tattoo across your back depicting a cobra eating your ex-boyfriend.

♥ Be comfortable in your lingerie. Men will think you're sexy if you feel sexy. So wear whatever underwear and/or lingerie will make you feel the most at ease when you're wearing it . . . and nothing else.

The final piece of the puzzle is figuring out where to go: his place or yours. From the guy's point of view, either place can work.

If he invites you to his place, he's hoping you'll be comfortable with that idea. Even if his place is usually a bit of a mess, he's going to have cleaned it up (at least a little bit) if he's inviting you over for the night. And whatever you do, don't complain about his bed. There's a time and a place to comment on the thread count of his sheets, but it's not while you're making out on them. What a turn off! If his bed is terrible, you can go to your place next time (and the time after that, and the time after that . . .).

That said, the first night together tends to be at the woman's place, because (a) a woman is a bit more relaxed in her own home and (b) women's places tend to be more comfortable than guys' places.

If he's coming over to your place, there are three things you should try to keep under control:

1. **Your mess.** You don't have to be Martha Stewart. But, ideally, every piece of clothing you own should not be on the floor of your bedroom.

2. **Your roommate.** Ask your roommate to have a little tact. Or, better yet, ask her to stay out really late that night. And if your roommate happens to be a guy, don't go to your place. Trust me—your date will assume that you're sleeping together because that's what he would want to be doing if he was your roommate! So it's best to avoid that awkward situation altogether.

3. **Your pet.** Maybe the most important thing of all. Having your cat/dog/ferret attack him while he's getting nude is NEVER adorable or cute. Play it safe and put the pet in another room for the night.

The bottom line is that the guy wants you to be comfortable. Whatever place you prefer is going to be good for him.

It's Show Time!

Once the two of you find yourselves in the bedroom, it's important to remember that men want the same thing you do: an orgasm. Just kidding!

Obviously, men want that, but that wasn't the point I was going to make. Instead, what I was going to say is that he wants to feel like you're attracted to him sexually . . . in exactly the same way that you hope he is attracted to you.

"If things click, curiosity and desire seem to take over."
—Roger, Baltimore, MD

Remember: We're not talking about a one night stand situation here. This is a guy who's been out on several dates with you. He's taking the relationship very seriously.

How do you make him feel relaxed and comfortable? Here are some tips:

♥ No laughing at him! The first time you see him naked is not the moment to be making any jokes, no matter how good-natured or clever they are. The chances of him taking it the wrong way are about 3,000 percent.

♥ This isn't a hostage negotiation. I said no laughing at him, but that doesn't mean no laughing at all. You can have fun. You're not Laurence Olivier playing Hamlet.

♥ Don't make a big deal about the lighting. If you're overly adamant about lights on or lights off, it's weird. Just light a few candles, turn down the lights, and everything will be fine.

♥ Have honesty and confidence about your past experiences. Whatever you've done or haven't done sexually in your life up to this point, be proud of it. Whether you're very experienced or more of a novice, it's okay. Don't worry about the guy being impressed. He won't get stressed out about your past if you don't.

♥ If he wants to do something you're not into, decline politely. Hopefully, you know this guy well enough that he's not going to give you some really bizarre request like asking you to speak with a foreign accent (trust me—I've heard it all!). But the fact is that you never know what turns people on until you're in the bedroom. Don't do anything that will compromise your comfort level—you'll hate yourself later (or during). However, you don't have to hit him, burst into tears, or get dressed and storm out of the place. Just tell him you'd rather not, and he'll gladly move on to stuff you are comfortable with. And if he's foolish enough to make a big stink about it, then lay down the law: he shapes up, or he's out the door.

A quick word about *your* body. Everyone has insecurities about how they look, and, obviously, when a guy is seeing you naked for the first time, there's a tendency for the stress to quadruple. The most important thing to remember is that none of it matters to the guy. If he was truly turned off by the size of your hips, he wouldn't be sleeping with you.

Now, if you have a particularly unusual scar or a bright red birthmark, he may ask you about it afterward. If that happens, just tell him the truth. He's not being accusatory; he's just curious. And believe me, he's got something about his body that drives him crazy as well: a mole, a gross toenail, or unwanted hair somewhere on his body. Use your imperfections as a bonding experience. Everyone's got them, and now that you're seeing each other naked, there's no point in trying to cover it up.

The rest of the night I leave to you. At this particular moment, your instincts will serve you better than I can. Have fun, enjoy it, and, most of all, *don't do anything you're uncomfortable with.* I'll tell you one thing: A smart, confident woman who knows what she likes and doesn't like in the bedroom is what turns men on the most.

How Was It for You?

Let's pick the action up after the magic show has ended. One of the first post-sex questions you'll be pondering is a timeless battle of the sexes issue:

Do men like to snuggle?

You're probably going to want to curl up next to guy for a bit after sex. But is that going to freak him out? Does he want you guys to go to opposite sides of the bed and not say a word?

Here's the answer: He's okay with a little caressing; he just doesn't want to do it until dawn. He's human, and like you, he wants to stay close to someone he's just been intimate with. But the three things he *doesn't* want are:

1. To feel pinned down for hours. More than likely, he's going to want to roll over and get some sleep at some point during the night. This doesn't mean he doesn't love you—it just means he's not seventeen years old.

2. To have an overly serious conversation about the relationship. In the guy's mind, you don't need to have this conversation—you just made love, so, hello, he's into you! Post-sex is a time to relax and be close, not to map out the next ten years of your life together.

3. To listen to you talk on your cell phone. How many times in this book have I said this? Well, I can't stress it

enough. Don't take a cell phone call in the middle of the night unless it's an emergency. If it's just a crazy friend calling, let it go to voice mail. Don't even pick up and tell them, "It's not a good a time to talk," because that's the understatement of the year.

Now, many women read the above advice and assume the following:

Okay, if he doesn't want to curl up all night, that means he doesn't want to spend the rest of the night here, right?

No. The guy wants to stay, and it's really awkward if you don't let him. Kicking him out (or leaving, if you're at his place) will make the guy feel like you're running away from him—literally! There's been a lot of buildup to this night, and he wants it to last.

Now, obviously, you need to part ways eventually. What guys want in this situation is sort of tricky. They need confirmation that you enjoyed yourself but reassurance that you aren't expecting to elope the following weekend.

So how do you communicate that message to him? If you're at his place, the most important decision is *when* you should leave. In general, you want to leave early, but not too early.

If you leave before 6 a.m., it sends the message of "the sun's up; I just got a good look at you; I really have to go." If you leave after 9 a.m., you're getting in the way of his day. So the perfect range is between 6 a.m. and 9 a.m. It says, "I don't really want this to end, but I understand that I don't live here."

If he's spent the night at your place, the trick is not to hustle him out the door. Or, at least, not to make him feel like he's being hustled out the door even if that's what needs to be done.

If he's sticking around longer than you want and you've got stuff to do, tell him you had an amazing time, you want to see him soon, but unfortunately . . .

♥   . . . you've got work you have to get to today

OR

♥   . . . you told your friend you'd have brunch with her and her mom

OR

♥   . . . if you don't run some errands today you'll be brushing your teeth with soap by tomorrow night.

He'll take the hint. He's got a life too. So give him a hug, and a good, long kiss, and send him on his way.

I've got news for you, though: Women find they have the *opposite* problem the morning after sex.

Janis, my issue isn't having a guy stick around too long. Instead, he's up and gone by first light. You just told me not to do that to him if we're at his place, so what should I do if he bolts on me?

Let him go. He likely has a legit excuse. In fact, you yourself may have to use one of these excuses at some point:

Reasons One of You May Head Home Early After Your First Night Together

♥   You have a breakfast meeting.
♥   You don't have any change of clothes, so you need to leave extra time to run home before work.

♥ You may sleep better in your own bed and need to grab an hour or two of sleep before going to work.

♥ You're leaving on a business trip that day.

♥ You're feeling allergic to the cat in the room and need to leave so you can breathe.

Even if he doesn't offer a reason, there's no point in making a big fuss. He'll probably figure out that he made a mistake and stay longer the next time. And if he doesn't, then you can tell he's acting weird.

Of course, there's one scenario that I haven't mentioned yet:

Janis, what if we both want to spend the next day together?

Then go have fun! Some couples just click extremely fast, and it's beyond awesome if you both feel like you want to have breakfast in bed.

If he asks to spend the day together and you don't want to, just remember my earlier tips for how to part ways smoothly. The conversation should go something like this:

Him: Want to go grab some breakfast?

You: I'd love to, but I actually told my friend I'd go wedding dress shopping with her.

Him: Oh.

You: Don't worry. I'd rather be having coffee with you. [*You give him a kiss.*]

You: And thank you for not freaking out when I said the words "wedding dress."

Him: No problem. Even though I'm a guy, I'm actually aware of the fact that people, on occasion, do get married.

You: Next time, we'll do breakfast afterward.
Him: Deal.

See? It couldn't be easier.

The Reconnect

Once you've parted ways, there's still one more hurdle to cross: how and when you should reconnect.

In the last chapter, Janis, you said that after the second date, I have carte blanche to call him. So, now, after we've had sex, I can just call him whenever I want, right?

Well . . . yes and no. You certainly have the right to pick up the phone and give him a ring whenever you feel like it. But my recommendation is that you give the guy a chance to call you. There's a certain coyness that comes from letting him make the first call after sex. It puts you in driver's seat. Don't worry: You'll come across as provocative, not disinterested.

However, if you haven't heard from him by the end of the next day, there's no need to play it cool forever. You're adults who have just slept together. You're allowed to communicate. The dilemma is how best to do it.

Post-Sex Communication Method	Pro	Con
E-mail	It says, "I may be having a busy day at work, but I'm still thinking about last night."	It can also say, "I am now communicating to you via memorandum."
Work phone	If it's a weekday, he'll be at that phone number all day.	Unless he's in meetings. In which case, you're leaving an intimate message on a corporate voice mail system. Or, even worse, his assistant may pick up the phone.
Cell phone	No matter where he is, he can pick up.	At the moment the call is placed, one of you is trying to parallel park a car and the other is in a place where the reception stinks. The call is an unmitigated disaster.
Home phone	If he's home, there will be few distractions and you can have a proper conversation.	If he's not home, it could be hours until he checks his home voice mail.
Unannounced visit	Screw the phone. What's better than live contact?	He'll think you're stalking him. Seriously.

In the end, I recommend one of the phone options, because e-mail is a little impersonal right after sex and the unannounced visit is dangerous.

When you guys do finally connect, let me warn you about two common mistakes women make:

Mistake #1

Now that we've slept together, I can be more erotic on the phone.
No. You don't have to give a detailed play-by-play of the night you slept together, because—hello!—he was there. He'll be thrilled to hear that you're still thinking about that night, but he doesn't need to have phone sex with you, since you've already done the real thing. Be excited, but don't be gross.

Mistake #2

If I try to make plans with him, he'll think I'm too desperate. I should just tell him how much fun I had and then get off the phone.
If you do that, he'll think you don't want to continue the relationship. He's hoping that you do want to see him again and, if he doesn't do it first, he's expecting you to ask when that can happen. If you don't, he'll think that he didn't deliver the goods when you guys made love and he'll run away and hide.

If you don't want to see him again, then don't make plans. But if you do decide to call him, you don't need to play games. We're WAY past that point now.

Not What You're After

Post-sex is one of the easiest times to tell if you're with the wrong kind of guy. Obviously, you want a guy who desires you even more *after* he's been with you. So if he suddenly seems distant or disconnected, it may be because he is. Give him some time to redeem himself, but if that attitude continues, don't you dare waste any more time on him!

The opposite extreme should also raise a warning flag. It's fabulous if he enjoyed making love to you (and with good reason! You're the best!). But you don't want sex to suddenly become his only interest. If he starts backing away from daytime activities, deep conversation, or an extended curiosity about your life, watch out. Sex is part of the relationship, but it's not everything.

Let Him Down Easy

If you decide after your first night together that the guy isn't right for you, try waiting a few days before breaking the bad news. You don't want it to seem like you're breaking up just because he's bad in bed (even if that's the case).

Now, you never, ever have to have mercy sex, but breaking up with a guy when he's in the shower the next morning will set his confidence back a good five years. He's the right match for someone, even if it's not you. But if you dump him five minutes after sex, he won't be a good match for anyone for quite a long time.

CHAPTER 7

Don't Call Them Groomsmen

Meeting Each Other's Friends

Now that you've been on several dates and spent the night together, this relationship is for real. It will soon be time to meet each other's friends. Obviously, you may have met some friends already—you may have even been set up by a mutual one. But now you have to take it to another level. It's not enough to know the names and faces of each other's friends—you need to spend some time together so you can get to know them and vice versa.

> *When do we meet each other's friends? If it's too early, it feels like I'm rushing the relationship. And if it's too late, it feels like one of us has something to hide.*

Yes, it's tricky, but not as tricky as you think. Meeting each other's friends isn't nearly as stressful as meeting each other's families. If you've been out a couple of times, it's normal to show him that you're not a hermit. Men *want* to meet your friends because they're important to you. They're also a reflection of you as a person.

"You need to see the type of people she hangs around early on so you can add that to the information you are collecting on her to make up your mind."
— Sean, Los Angeles, CA

Some guys have told me that they want to meet your friends by date number five. Others have said they want to do it after you've had sex, because then you're really "an item." My opinion? After about date number four, you're good to go.

The Meeting Process

The most important thing men are looking for when they meet your friends—and this I can't stress enough—is to *not be overwhelmed*. Many women try to do too much too quickly. Here are two classic mistakes:

1. You have some sort of massive event that features twenty-five of your closest friends . . . and him.

2. Every time the two of you go out, you bring along a different one of your friends.

Men like to be eased in. Here's how you can do that:

♥ Start with your closest friends. If the first person your boyfriend meets is a female friend from college who you see two times a year, he's going to be confused. Why is he meeting this random person? Pick out your two or three closest friends and start with them.

♥ Save your male friends for later (unless they're married). Trust me—it's just easier this way. Lots of single women have single guy friends, but it's inevitably more complicated when your boyfriend meets them. Your boyfriend will assume that your male friend is secretly in love with you and wants to have sex with you (because at one point in his life, your boyfriend had female friends that he secretly wanted to sleep with). The longer you've been together, the more secure your boyfriend will feel, and the easier that meeting will be. Oh, and by the way, if you happen to be friendly with an ex-boyfriend, I think it goes without saying that you should save him for last (if at all).

♥ If possible, one or two friends at a time. Yes, there are circumstances where meeting a bunch of friends at once is unavoidable—you happen to be having a large birthday party very soon into the relationship, for example. But, in general, small groups work best. That way, your boyfriend will actually get to know each of your friends (which is, after all, the point) and he won't feel like an outsider as you guys reminisce about high school.

♥ Schedule events with your friends that involve some sort of activity. If everyone is just sitting around in your living room, there's a chance the guy may feel like he's being interviewed. It's far more fun to go to a movie and have dinner afterward. That way, there's a built-in activity, and if you run out of stuff to talk about at dinner, you can always discuss the movie you just saw.

But by far the biggest mistake that women make when in-
troducing their new boyfriend to their friends is:

♥ Don't send your friends to do your dirty work. It's so
    backhanded and tacky. Men HATE this! If you're un-
    happy with him, talk to him yourself. If your friends are
    doing your complaining for you, he'll feel like the sense
    of trust between the two of you has been completely vi-
    olated. This holds true throughout the relationship.
    Obviously, your friends are going to be on their best
    behavior the first time around. But don't ever turn
    them into messengers if there's a bump in the relation-
    ship. Your friends can help, but you've always got to
    lead the way.

Feedback Time

Once the meeting has concluded, you're then faced with
feedback: Your friends will tell you what they think of your
boyfriend and vice versa. Here's what a lot of women think:

*It's totally fine to let my boyfriend hear what my friends think
of him no matter what they say. I mean, we're all adults here,
right?*

False. Obviously, if your friends have nothing but praise for
your new guy, that's great and he'll be glad to hear it. But
sometimes your friends may make an observation in passing
that just doesn't need to be passed on.

Observations Your Friends May Make About Your Boyfriend That You Don't Need to Share with Him

"He's not as tall as I thought he'd be."

"He went to the bathroom a lot. Did he have indigestion?"

"He seemed nervous."

"He had something in his teeth."

"I thought he'd be more sophisticated."

It's not that your friends' opinions don't matter, but, seriously, what good would come from telling your boyfriend that he's shorter than your friends thought he would be? How does he respond to that? I'm not saying you should lie. I'm just saying that if your boyfriend asks what your friends thought of him, you should accentuate the positive comments.

But Janis, what if my friends have a more serious criticism about my boyfriend, like telling me they don't think we're a good match. What do I do then?

The first thing you should do is tell your friends to hold their friggin' horses! After one or two meetings with your boyfriend, it's a little early to be delivering that sort of message!

Even if you and your boyfriend have been together a while,

it still doesn't make sense to relay all of your friends' critiques. Why? *Because your friends' comments are only valid if you agree with them.*

If your friends tell you that your boyfriend should let you speak more in conversations, you need to take that information and decide (a) if you think that's true and (b) if it's something you want to change. If so, then you should absolutely have that conversation with your boyfriend. But if you just tell your boyfriend, "My friends think you don't let me talk enough in conversations," I guarantee his response will be, "Well, what do you think?" If you haven't decided what you think, then he's going to wonder why you're having this conversation with him in the first place.

There's also a completely different type of feedback that I haven't mentioned yet—namely, what your boyfriend thinks of your friends.

It's important to men that you let them express their opinion about your friends.

Every single client I surveyed about this issue said they want to be honest with you when talking about your friends. Don't worry: He's not a moron. He won't make a deeply insulting comment about someone you've known forever. Letting him speak his mind shows that you value his opinion, and that's very important to guys (as it should be with you as well).

Now, what sort of comments from your boyfriend are, in fact, appropriate? Consider the following chart:

Fair Comment	Creepy Comment
Your friend Sarah talks a lot. I had trouble getting a word in edgewise with her.	Your friend Sarah wouldn't shut up and said some really shallow and stupid things.
I see what you mean about Anna—she has a very flirtatious demeanor.	Anna is unbelievably sexy and hot, huh? I couldn't take my eyes off her.
Is Kelly getting over a recent breakup?	Wow—is Kelly a man-hating bitch or what?
Wendy seemed a little shy.	Wendy needs to get laid so she can loosen up.
I got sort of an unusual vibe from Megan.	She's totally a lesbian and she doesn't know it.
Liz is really fabulous. Let's hang out with her again.	I was pleasantly surprised to hear that Liz is single. Wow—watch a catch she is, huh?

You get the idea—there are some comments that are way over the line. And you can absolutely get annoyed if he makes those sorts of remarks.

The Dudes

Now that your boyfriend has successfully met your friends (phew!), it's time to move on to phase two: meeting his friends. This moment is one the guy will be excited about.

When you're meeting his friends, you've reached a very important moment. If his friends don't think you're the right match, the rest of the relationship is suddenly an uphill battle. Obviously, the same holds true with you and your friends, but it's even more significant with a guy and his buddies. Why? Because your friends will secretly give the guy a grade ("He's a B-plus. Not bad, but she could do a little better.") A guy's friends, however, tend to grade only Pass/Fail, because they're usually just happy their buddy has found someone. (Also, grading Pass/Fail requires less effort.)

So the good news is that the guy's friends are easier graders than your friends. But the bad news is that if they do fail you, you're really screwed. Since they don't hand out a lot of failing grades, your boyfriend is *really* going to take notice if they do.

So how do you ensure that his friends get the right impression? Well, first and foremost is the golden rule:

NO FLIRTING WITH HIS BUDDIES!

Many women get into trouble because they try to be overly charming when they meet their boyfriend's friends. That's all well and good, but you need to make *very* sure you stay on the safe side of the line. The minute you go too far and start coming on to his friends, your new boyfriend will quickly turn into your ex-boyfriend.

It's also possible that one of his friends starts hitting on you. It's flattering, but also very uncomfortable for you (and your boyfriend!). So what should you do? First and foremost, *don't flirt back*. I think I've already explained why.

You should also *tell your boyfriend*. There is a strict code among guys about hitting on each other's girlfriends, and if someone violates this code, no one will stand for it. If you tell your boyfriend, it will be dealt with immediately.

Here are a couple of other things guys hope you will keep in mind when meeting his friends for the first time:

♥ Don't talk about children, marriage, where you're going to be living together in five years, and/or whether you'll be taking his last name. This advice was important on the first date and it's still important now. Talking about kids will cause your boyfriend's friends to freak out. And then they'll tell your boyfriend and it will freak him out. Even if your relationship is on the fast track, it's still safe to stay clear of all these topics during this initial get-together.

♥ Try not to talk about sex. In an attempt to have guys think you're cool, many women decide that they will bring up sex as a topic of conversation. Don't get me wrong—guys love to talk about sex. And they're even happy to talk about it with a stranger. But when that stranger is their buddy's girlfriend, it's really awkward for everyone involved.

♥ If you're not a sports fan, don't talk about sports. It's a sweet sentiment to try to discuss a conversation topic that guys enjoy. However, if you don't know what you're talking about, you'll quickly be excluded from the conversation, while the guys talk about fantasy football for the next three thousand hours.

♥ Don't physically hide behind your boyfriend. This sounds like something you'd never do, but I see it happen ALL THE TIME! When women get nervous in these situations, they tend to grab their boyfriend's arm and sort of hide behind it. Or they feel the need to continuously cuddle with their boyfriend throughout dinner. A little affection between you and boyfriend is natural and nice. But you also need to remember that you're not in the bedroom; you're in a public place, interacting with his friends. So at a certain point, drop the cuddling and engage in the conversation.

And, most important of all:

♥ Be nice. It's how you'd want him to be with your friends, right? Even if you're not crazy about his buddies, they get the benefit of the doubt the first time around.

As for feedback from you about his friends, the rules are basically the same as when he met your friends: He wants to know your opinion, and you should give it. But don't be overly harsh after only one meeting. If his friends rub you the wrong way over and over again, then you should have a conversation with your boyfriend about that. But after the first meeting, try to treat his buddies with the same respect that you'd want him to show to your close friends.

It's also important not to keep score. The number of nights that you go out with his friends does not need to exactly equal the number of nights he went out with your friends. It may take four separate events for you to meet his close friends, while he was able to meet yours in only two nights. That's okay. Your love of each other should be exactly equal; the number of nights you socialize with each other's friends doesn't have to be.

Now, there's one additional situation I haven't talked about yet:

What if his best friend is a woman?

Needless to say, this can be very tricky. Your head is going to immediately fill up with questions like:

- ♥ Have the two of you dated?
- ♥ Are the two of you still kind of dating?
- ♥ Even if you haven't dated, have you two slept together?
- ♥ Is she secretly (or not so secretly!) in love with you?
- ♥ Are you secretly (or not so secretly!) in love with her?

Obviously, that last question is very important. If you suddenly get the feeling that you're a consolation prize and your boyfriend's heart is really with someone else, you need to sit down and have a talk, pronto!

But, that situation aside, you've got to give your boyfriend the benefit of the doubt for now. If you start issuing ultimatums and demand that he hangs out only with his male friends, you're going to seem jealous and psycho. You need to be confident enough in the relationship that you're not worried when your boyfriend talks to other women. If you're that insecure, it's means the relationship is already broken.

Now, that said, you're allowed to ask the obvious questions, just don't go all CIA style when you do it. You have a right to know if there's a romantic history with him and this other woman . . . but don't give your boyfriend a look of death when he provides the answer. If they have dated, remember: It's in the past. He's dating you now. And if she's secretly in love with him, that's her problem. He would have dated her by now if he was interested.

After a few months, you can and should address any red flags that haven't gone away. If he gets you a bottle of Chardonnay for Christmas and gets her a beautiful pair of earrings, that's a problem. Or, if this female friend is so jealous of you that it's become really awkward to socialize with her, say something. If your boyfriend is serious about the relationship, he'll do whatever's necessary to make you feel comfortable. And if he's always putting this other woman's interests ahead of yours, it's time for him to change his ways or get a new girlfriend.

After the Fact

Once you've met each other's friends, there's something you have to remember:

> IT'S CRUCIAL TO STILL HAVE TIME ALONE FOR JUST THE TWO OF YOU EVEN AFTER YOU'VE MET EACH OTHER'S FRIENDS.

Every time I tell women that piece of advice, here's what they say:

> *You don't need to remind me of that, Janis! I'm not going to forget that we still need alone time.*

Seriously—that's what every woman says. But what you don't realize is that it actually requires effort on your part to have alone time. It can be hard to find nights to get together as you balance work, family, and the rest of your lives with your relationship. And now that you have the added element of each other's friends, it's even more difficult. There's always going to be someone who's going to a movie, having a dinner party, or heading to the bar at the corner for a drink. The instinct is to say yes to all of these activities.

But sooner or later you have to say no. Men need time alone for just the two of you. Being out in a big group is fun, but it also requires a lot of work—especially if you're hanging out with people you're still getting to know. Going out just the two of you is usually more relaxing and more romantic.

If your boyfriend plans an event for the two of you, don't then invite your friends along. It sounds so obvious, but I've actually seen women do it, which makes me put my face in my hands and think, "Girlie, what are you DOING?!" Needless to say, a romantic dinner isn't nearly as romantic if there are five people at the table. And don't make it impossible to have these romantic nights by completely filling the social calendar up a month ahead of time. You've got to leave some holes for him to plan stuff.

Part of being a couple is learning to check with each other before making plans. Best rule of thumb: There are two nights on the weekend. So spend one night with friends and one alone.

Not What You're After

Be very, very careful about men who hide their friends from you. There are lots of reasons for this, and almost all of them are bad:

- ♥ He's afraid you'll think his friends are terrible people.
- ♥ He *knows* his friends are terrible people, but he's too lazy to get better friends.

♥ He has a commitment phobia, and doesn't want you to get too close to the people he cares about.
♥ He likes to overly compartmentalize his life.
♥ Your opinion on his friends isn't important to him.

If you're going to be part of his life, he needs to be comfortable sharing his friends with you. If he's not, then I wonder what else is going to make him squeamish down the line.

And it's just as bad if he has no interest in meeting your friends. He can be uncomfortable at the idea of going out with all your sorority sisters on date number two, but sooner or later he needs to acknowledge the importance of your friends. If he doesn't, then he's not taking you seriously and he needs to go.

Let Him Down Easy

It's important not to share too many embarrassing details about your new guy with your friends, even if it's done in good spirits. Why? Because if you split up, your gossip may really come back to haunt him.

Let me give you an example. Let's say your new boyfriend makes a funny noise when he orgasms. Hey—it happens! It certainly doesn't make him a bad guy; it's just sort of a funny quirk. So, naturally, you gossip about it with a few of your friends. Fine. But if you have loose lips and then dump the guy, he's going to be embarrassed to learn that half the women he goes out with on dates now know about his orgasm sound. There are some details that should just stay in the bedroom.

CHAPTER 8

Romantic Mondays
The Casual Moments of the Relationship

Relationships aren't just dinner dates and sex (hopefully that isn't a newsflash!). What makes a bond last is when you guys still love each other during the downtime of the relationship—a night at home watching TV, a Sunday morning spent lounging around the house, a get-together that hasn't been planned within an inch of its life. In short, the difference between someone you're sleeping with and someone you're dating boils down to this: Can you relax around each other?

Ideally, casual time should happen naturally. A sign of a good relationship is when you just sort of find yourself having a mellow night at home watching a DVD as opposed to one of you robotically saying to the other, "We have been together for 2.5 weeks. Commence casual evening program."

In general, guys will ease into the casual phase of the relationship at a slower pace than women. Part of this is chivalry—there is an inherent need in a lot of men to take you out on the town. The last thing he wants you to think is that he's cheap or lazy. Also, it feels safer to have a concrete plan. It gives the date a clear beginning, middle, and end, and that's reassuring.

Sooner or later, though, your boyfriend will realize that the relationship isn't a business convention—you don't need an itinerary for every waking moment.

He'll get there. I promise. So don't worry if, at first, he doesn't want to come over to your place every night of the week to hang out and spend the night. He'll probably want to start with once or twice a week and build from there.

Now, let me add a crucial piece of advice:

> How you act on the nights you're NOT together is just as important as the nights you are together.

Obviously, you shouldn't be getting it on with other men when you have a night off from your boyfriend (if you haven't figured that out by now, go back to the beginning of the book and start over!).

Instead, the dilemma is whether it's a good idea to call your boyfriend and chit-chat on a night when you're not seeing each other.

By this point on the relationship, a guy will be happy to have you check in with him every day because (a) he obviously likes you and (b) who doesn't like the idea of someone thinking about them when they're apart?

That said, there are some major cautions to abide by:

Caution #1: Don't call and tell him you have a quick story . . . and then keep him on the phone for forty-five minutes. Long, involved stories are far more satisfying in person with a glass of wine than they are over the phone.

Caution #2: Don't play seven thousand rounds of phone tag. You're not seeing each other tonight, but you're probably seeing each other tomorrow night. So there's no need to drive yourselves crazy trying if the telecommunication gods aren't on your side today.

Caution #3: Don't go into whisper voice mode. You know what I'm talking about! This is when you call up your boyfriend and start whispering softly how much you miss him. If you love him and miss him, say it normally like you mean it!

Caution #4: Don't call him and not talk to him. This is beyond annoying for guys. You check in, chat for a bit, and then the conversation has reached its logical end, but you just sort of keep him on the phone because you don't want to hang up. So, instead, you talk about nothing. Or, in some cases, you don't even talk at all—you just sort of stay on the phone in silence. Yuck! You're not a teenager. Call him. Have a conversation. Then end the call.

And, most importantly:

Caution #5: Don't turn the call into a guilt trip about the fact that you aren't seeing each other tonight. That's going to leave a sour taste in his mouth and make the next time you're together more tense. If he's going on a date with another woman, that's a problem. If he's going to a work dinner without you, give him a break.

It's also possible that the tables will be turned. The guy could call you on an off night just to chat and you may be the one who's busy at work or in the middle of doing something else. That's not a problem . . . as long as you call him back. You MUST do this.

Even if you don't have time to talk for long and even if you're seeing each other tomorrow, you've still got to call him back today and let him know what you're up to. If you don't, his feelings will be hurt. Men talk a big game, but deep inside, they're softies.

Together Again

When the two of you do eventually get together for a casual evening, it doesn't really matter whether you go to his place or yours. If, however, you find that you guys are favoring one place over another, the next big question is:

When can you leave a toothbrush at his place?

It's amazing how much a toothbrush symbolizes. It's because you both know the toothbrush is the first small step on the road to living together.

Most of my clients say that after the third night together, you can ask to keep some toiletries at his place (and he can do the same at your place). Just don't go over the top. A few basics—deodorant, toothbrush, shampoo—will have to suffice for now. There's no need to bring twelve bottles of moisturizer and a vanity full of makeup at this point.

And, by the way, it's worth having a sense of what guys consider "casual" activities so that you're on the same page:

Casual Activities That Guys Enjoy Doing with Their Girlfriend

♥ Take-out food plus TV night. This is an all-time favorite. A little trashy TV and some Chinese take-out is a cornerstone of most relationships.

♥ Whipping up a quick dinner at home. In the same ballpark as take-out food—throw some burgers on the grill, pop in a movie, and you're home free.

♥ Taking the dogs for a long walk. No matter what the weather, this is just a great way to get some fresh air and be together (with Rover).

♥ Weekend leisure time. You wake up together on a Saturday morning and realize that neither of you has much planned that day. So what's better than spending a chunk of the day with each other? Grab a bite, take a walk, go to a museum . . . the world is your oyster!

♥ Getting a present for someone (besides you). Obviously, he loves getting you gifts. But he has a mother (and probably a sister) too, and they have birthdays. He struggles every year to find them something they'll like, and any female advice you can offer will be much appreciated.

♥ Working out. This is easy if the two of you already belong to the same gym or go jogging on the same route in the park. It doesn't work as well if one of you likes to go rock climbing and the other one likes to ride the stationary bike at the gym.

On the flip side, there are also a few casual activities that you probably think your boyfriend will want to do with you, but, in reality . . .

Casual Activities That Guys Prefer to Do *Without* Their Girlfriend

♥ Routine errands. Yes, being with you would make these mundane activities more fun. But it will also make them take much longer. And before you argue with me, I'll give you one word: drugstore. The average man can be in and out in two minutes. After two minutes, you're still looking for a shopping cart to carry all the stuff you're going to buy.

♥ Hanging out while he's got work to do. Some nights, your boyfriend is going to be swamped with work and he needs to come home and get stuff done. On those nights, he generally won't feel comfortable if you come over—even if you tell him that you're just going to sit quietly in the corner and read a book. He'll be stressed because he wishes he could be entertaining you. At this point in the relationship, men still prefer to do their work one night and then go out with you the next. Yes, he can't compartmentalize his life forever, but he's not quite ready to merge everything together.

♥ Rearranging stuff at his place. A lot of guys have had the bookshelf in the same corner since the day they moved in. If he wanted to move something, he'd move it. But he has everything where he likes it, so there's no need to discuss the matter further. You can offer ideas, but at the end of the day, he's probably not going to do anything. Rearranging stuff relaxes many women, but it makes most guys get annoyed. And if you insist on moving furniture it will make him feel like you've decided to move in—even though he hasn't asked you to do that yet.

♥ Buying electronics. He already knows what he wants. And he doesn't want you to know how much it costs because you'll think he's insane.

♥ Anything having to do with his car. See above section on electronics.

The Two Major Exceptions

There are two leisure activities that I haven't discussed yet because they don't really fit into any of the categories above. Instead, they require their own special analysis.

Exception #1: The Sporting Life

The first exception is something you'll have to deal with soon into the relationship: watching sports. And the question that will no doubt pop into your mind is:

Does he want me to watch sports with him?

The truth is that it doesn't matter. If you're a sports fan, he'll be happy to bond with you over that topic. And if you're not, no worries. It's not a deal breaker in a relationship if you don't like sports.

What matters to guys is simply that you are cool with the fact that he's a sports fan. Your interest can come and go. But as long as you don't mind that he likes to check the baseball score before he heads to bed each night, everything is golden.

Now, is it possible that he can get a little carried away with his sports-watching hobby? Absolutely.

Okay, Janis, I have no problem with the fact that my boyfriend likes to watch sports. But sometimes it just consumes his life, and, therefore, mine as well. How long is he allowed to sulk after his team loses before I tell him to get over it? Is he going to freak out if I schedule social plans during the NBA playoffs, which, incidentally, last two and a half months?

These are totally legitimate questions. Even guys themselves will admit that they can get carried away with their passion for sports—especially after a heartbreaking loss by their favorite team.

So if they've gone too far with their passion—tell them. If they've been moping around for a week after their team lost in the Super Bowl, you can let him know it's time to move on.

Most guys have binged on ESPN for the past decade, and know it's okay to miss the Masters to spend time with someone they love (unless Tiger Woods is winning). If a particular event is really important to your boyfriend—he's a lifelong Milwaukee Brewers fan and they're playing in the World Series—he'll let you know. And if he says that every event is really important, then you should let him know he's being ridiculous.

Exception #2: Clothes Make the Man

Shopping for clothes is the second activity that guys want to do with you some of the time. Obviously, I'm not talking about clothes for you. I think we can agree that you'd both be miserable if he went with you on those trips.

I'm talking about buying clothes for him. Many women wonder:

Does my boyfriend want my input on his wardrobe?

The answer is yes. Even the most fashion savvy guy will be happy to take wardrobe advice from you because he knows that you have better fashion taste than he does.

Even if clothes aren't really your thing, there's still a 99 percent chance you're going to have more style than he does. Most of the time, he's in desperate need of some help, and he's thrilled to have you rescue him.

What's the best way to dive in? One thing to keep in mind is the earlier section about sports.

"Remember, we're guys . . . we don't want to shop during the playoffs."

—Charlie, New York, NY

Fair enough. But during those times that the playoffs aren't on (all two weeks of them), here are two different strategies you can use to help your boyfriend improve his wardrobe:

Strategy #1 (Less Intense): Occasional Commentary

This is the easiest method. All your boyfriend has to do is wear the clothes he already owns and you provide your insight.

The thing to remember here is *not to go over the top*. If you provide a running commentary for every outfit every day, he's just going to tune you out. You've got to pick and choose your battles.

When you do make a comment, guys like it if you can have a positive spin. Why? He knows he may need *some* help with his wardrobe, but he thinks he isn't a total fashion disaster. If you completely burst his bubble (even if it's beyond justified), he may not be able to handle it.

Here are a few examples of how you can put things gently but still get your point across:

Too Harsh	Just Right
That sweater you're wearing is so out of style that I want to burn it when you take it off.	You'd look handsome in a new black V-neck!
You've put on so much weight since you've gotten those pants that they just look ridiculous on you.	Those pants look like they've served you well, but maybe we should go to The Gap and get you a nice new pair—I think chinos are on sale this week!
Sneakers? With that outfit?	You know what—I think those brown shoes you have in your closet would go perfectly with what you have on. Do you want to try them on?
When you wear that jacket you look like a bum.	Hmmm . . . there's a huge hole in your jacket. Let's go buy a new one. Or, at the very least, let's patch the old one.
That T-shirt is a bio hazard.	Bleach works well for armpit stains.
Navy suit, white shirt, red tie. Bor-ring.	You see that guy wearing the French blue shirt with the pink tie? What do you think of that? It's bold and also kind of amazing, right?

Remember: just because he wants your help doesn't mean you should destroy his self-confidence. That will do neither of you any good.

Strategy #2 (More Intense): He Brings You Along When He Goes Clothes Shopping

Sometimes it will actually be okay for you to accompany your boyfriend while he goes clothes shopping. I mean, if you're encouraging him to buy a new sweater, why wouldn't he want to take you along to help him pick one out. It's really a great bonding moment in the relationship.

The good news is that he doesn't expect you to pay for his clothes (you're not his mom). The bad news is that he's going to get tired of this activity a lot quicker than you will. So you've got to spend your time wisely:

Things to Keep in Mind If You Go Shopping for Clothes with Your Boyfriend

1. Let him pick the stores. Maybe, down the road, you can steer him into a new place. But for now, stick to the stores where he feels most comfortable.

2. Don't push him into buying things that are too crazy. If his style is preppy, then he doesn't need to get a new, urban look. Work within the confines of who he is. If you make him get stuff that is too bonkers, he'll never wear it.

3. Don't bad mouth his taste to the salespeople. This drives guys crazy. If he doesn't love a sweater that you

think he should get, let it go. Do NOT make some passive-aggressive remark to the salesperson like, "I like that sweater, but he's just going to stick to the same, boring stuff he always wears."

4. Don't force him to exceed his budget. If he's looking at a blazer that's ten bucks more than he wants to spend, that's one thing. But if he isn't prepared to drop $175 on a cashmere sweater, there's no need to make him feel cheap.

5. Don't turn it into a shopping trip for yourself. Yes, if you're at Banana Republic and you need to pick up a white T-shirt, that's okay. But the minute you have to try something on, you've lost him.

6. When he's had enough, let him stop. As I said, this moment will occur long before you'd call it quits if you were shopping for yourself. But you're not. You're shopping for him. And when he's done, he's done. You could walk by the most incredible outfit and he won't notice or care.

7. Let him deal with making room in his closet/dresser for the new clothes. He'll clean out his closet when he feels the time is right (or when it's so packed that he can't squeeze anything else in there). If you force him to go through everything now, or, even worse, if you start going through his closet on your own, it will end in a fight. It's not worth the aggravation.

Not What You're After

In the beginning of this chapter I advised you to give your boyfriend a little breathing room as he gets comfortable spending casual time with you. The flip side of that advice, though, is just as important: You should be concerned if there is no forward progress in the amount of casual time you spend together.

Easing into this phase of the relationship is fine . . . as long as the easing doesn't stop. If he's been coming over two nights a week for several months, he should be willing to go to three or four nights a week. And then he should stop counting. If he's reluctant to do that, watch out. Something's holding him back, and it's probably the fact that he doesn't want to commit emotionally.

Let Him Down Easy

This is one of the most important "Let Him Down Easy" sections in this whole book. Why? Because I'm advising you against an activity that seems like it would be totally fine.

Here it is: After you've broken up with a guy, you MUST cut off your casual time together. It probably seems like being friendly after the breakup would help let him (and yourself) down easy. But, in reality, the opposite is true. It's a lot easier for him if you make a clean break. This means avoiding long phone conversations where you tell each other funny stories from your day at work. That's cute, casual behavior when you're together; if you do it after you've split, you're only postponing the inevitable.

Now here's the real kicker: Even if he calls begging to hang out, don't accommodate him. At that point, he's a lovesick junkie. And while it may be hard for you to suppress your compassion and do nothing, that's exactly what you have to do in this situation. He'll get better and live to fight another day. But if you continue these casual activities with him, you're only supporting what has become a bad habit.

Part Three

The Happy Couple

CHAPTER 9

He Likes Scented Candles (He Just Won't Admit It)

A Romantic Weekend Trip Away

Men love romantic weekends away as much as women do. As far as he's concerned, you can take the trip even if you're not yet eternal soul mates.

So how soon into the relationship can I bring up the topic of a weekend away together?

He's ready when you're ready. Weekends away don't carry the same "oh-my-God-shes-wants-to-get-married-really-soon-and-that's-totally-scaring-me" connotation that talking about children or moving in together has.

First of all, romantic weekends are fun and relaxing. And who doesn't like that?

And, more importantly, *weekends away help speed up the getting-to-know-you process*. When you're with someone twenty-four hours a day, you learn a lot about them. This includes details you wouldn't necessarily learn on a date, such as:

♥ Does he need to wake up early and go for a run?
♥ How does he take his coffee?
♥ Does he eat a full breakfast or is he a cup of coffee and a muffin guy?

♥ Is he a complete and total slob in the room because he knows there's maid service?

♥ Does he tip the maid?

♥ Is he obsessive-compulsive about where his toiletries go? And will he share his toothpaste if you forgot yours?

♥ If there's a TV in the bedroom, will he turn on *SportsCenter* after sex?

♥ Is he patient with the hotel staff if something's out of place or does he turn into an instant man-diva?

The answers to these questions are neither "good" nor "bad." They're just important. You need to know these details to see if you're truly compatible with someone. You'll find out everything eventually, but a weekend away lets it happen quicker. And the sooner you know if you're right for each other, the faster the relationship can move forward.

STORY TIME

I set up a client named Ben with a woman named Hilary. They really hit it off. I mean . . . it was hot stuff right off the bat. Ben loved to travel, so fairly soon into the relationship, they were going away together on the weekends. That's when Hilary discovered that Ben is a disaster in the bathroom—let's just say he isn't all that clean. Some women would have no problem with this. But it drove Hilary up a wall. She mentioned this to Ben but he never changed his habits. For Hilary, it was a deal breaker. So they broke up, which is always unfortunate. But those weekends away let Hilary figure out fairly quickly that she and Ben just weren't soul mates.

The Setting

So where should you guys go? It should be a choice you make together. But I've got news for you: If you suggest a few places that you've been thinking about, your boyfriend will LOVE that. You're taking charge and it totally turns him on.

> *"It is a refreshing and welcome change if she plans the trip."*
>
> —Tim, Houston, TX

Where you go depends on your personal preferences—if neither of you likes sitting in the sun, then Palm Beach in July may not be the ideal spot! But in talking to my guys, it's clear that there are some types of trips that almost always work well:

♥ Wine Tasting. A big yes for men . . . just as long as neither of you gets depressed and/or angry when you drink too much red wine. If you don't live on the west coast, a trip to Napa or Sonoma is going to be expensive. (And even if you do live on the west coast, it's still expensive.) But there are local vineyards all over the United States. A trip out to the countryside to drink some Cabernet followed by a night at a local inn is a great option.

♥ Spa Weekend. Women are always surprised to see this as a possibility. Most guys secretly have wanted to try a spa but they would never, ever do it without a woman accompanying them. You're their excuse! The fact is that a massage, a steam, a nice dinner, and a relaxing hotel room sounds great to him. (Just please don't make him get a facial.)

♥ The Beach/Anywhere Warm. A great choice, especially if you live somewhere that isn't always sunny. There's no itinerary to worry about. You can just catch some rays, walk in the sand, and drink fruit-flavored cocktails with little umbrellas.

♥ A Great Hotel . . . Near or Far. Sometimes, the hotel itself can be the destination. Being in a hotel is inherently romantic because there's (a) room service and (b) maid service. And you don't even have to go far away. If, for example, if you both live in the suburbs of Chicago, there's nothing wrong with driving into the city and having a romantic weekend thirty minutes from where you live. The money you save on travel you can spend on champagne!

♥ Golf/Ski/Sailing/Other Sports-Themed Weekend. Guys love these kinds of weekends, but—here's the key part— they only want to do an activity you're both into. He has no interest in going golfing if you don't enjoy the sport. It's not very romantic for him to be hitting the links all day without you. He'll have plenty of time down the road to go golfing with his buddies. So don't suggest something you don't want to do just because you think it will make him happy. He'll be happy if you're enjoying the weekend as much as he is.

By the way, don't confuse an elaborate vacation for a weekend away. If you guys are comfortable taking a weeklong vacation together at this point, that's great. But most people prefer to crawl before they walk. Hawaii, Europe, and the Caribbean are all amazing trips, but guys prefer to build up to (and save up for) trips like that. Start with something simpler.

The Least Romantic Part of the Romantic Weekend

One of the most confusing issues you'll be confronted with after you pick a place is who pays for what.

If it's totally obvious that he wants to pay for the whole thing—he makes a ton of money and said, "I want to take you away for the weekend"—then you don't have to offer. Just enjoy yourself (and thank him afterward!).

If you're not sure whether he's planning to take you away or whether he wants you to contribute some money, then I'd play it safe and offer to pay for at least some of the weekend. Personally, I think the guy should ALWAYS pay for the whole trip. The weekend isn't about money; it's about spending time together. So if he's obsessing about who pays for what, it's a real buzz-kill. Even if his salary is modest, I think it's better to go somewhere inexpensive than to try to go to Vegas but make you pay for it.

> *"I would not care about paying for the weekend if it means I get the chance to know the woman better."*
> —Dan, Phoenix, AZ

Now, there are some situations where guys will let you contribute financially. However, you don't have to split the whole trip fifty-fifty. Instead, you can offer to pick up some part of the trip. If he's paying for the hotel, you can offer to pick up dinner. Yes, the hotel bill will probably be more expensive, but you're still contributing to the trip in a meaningful way.

> *What if he insists on paying for the whole thing? How much should I protest?*

You don't need to protest that hard. Offering to pay was nice, but most men were brought up right and will want to take you away for the weekend. So if it's clear that he wants to pay, you don't need to keep insisting on contributing because then things will be awkward.

Now, if he does pay for the whole weekend, try to avoid running up the bill. You don't need three spa treatments a day. Not every meal has to be room service. And, for the love of God, take it easy on the mini-bar!

Needless to say, you should thank him for paying for the weekend. And here's a great idea that one of my clients came up with:

> *"If he pays for a vacation of substantial cost, get him a little but thoughtful gift as a thank you."*
>
> —Nick, San Francisco, CA

I LOVE that idea. Honestly, I think you should do this no matter what the vacation costs. It's such a nice gesture that it will definitely make him want to go away with you again.

Putting the Romance in the Romantic Weekend

If he's picking up the bill for the weekend, then you're probably going to have the same concern you felt on the first date:

If I let him pay, isn't he expecting something sexual in return?

There is no sex quota that coincides with the room rate. If you're going away together for a weekend, you've probably already slept together. He didn't just take you away so he could get inside your pants because—pardon my bluntness—he's done that already!

So let's be realistic. He wants to have sex with you, but it's because it adds something special to the trip and says that the two of you have reached a nice comfort level in the relationship. I know it's a subtle distinction, but it's really important, so let me say it again: *He doesn't want sex as payback; rather, he just hopes it's something you want to do no matter who's paying and how much it costs.*

Sex isn't the only thing he's looking forward to over the course of the weekend. He wants what you want:

- ♥ No needless interruptions from business
- ♥ Lots of rest
- ♥ A romantic dinner
- ♥ Relaxing time together

That last item—relaxing time together—is actually more complicated that it sounds. This weekend away is probably the first time you two have been together for forty-eight hours in a row. Which leads to this question:

Okay, we don't want to do a golf trip because then he'd be golfing alone all day. But, that said, are we supposed to spend every waking minute together? Is it unromantic if I want two hours alone in the spa? Will he mind?

The goal of the weekend is to be together, but guys don't mind if you each have a little alone time. You don't have to be with each other every second of every day. Just remember the following:

1. Check with each other before scheduling activities for yourself. If you're going to the spa or checking out an art gallery, your boyfriend will probably want to come with you. At the very least, it's nice to give him the option. That way, he's not alone in the hotel room when the romantic room service dinner he orders arrives.

2. There is such a thing as too much alone time. Remember: The point of this weekend is to be together. Even if one of you is reading a book while the other takes a bath, it's nice to be relaxing in the same hotel room.

You can have a little alone time if you want, but keep it brief. You don't want to come home from a romantic weekend feeling like you haven't seen each other!

Next Time, Maybe a King Bed?

The final piece of advice in this chapter is, without question, the most important:

> DON'T COMPLAIN ABOUT THE HOTEL
> WHILE YOU ARE ON THE TRIP.

If he's paying for the hotel, then any moaning about the room is beyond rude. Even if you're splitting the cost, don't consider your half of the bill as a license to complain. You'll seem like a spoiled brat and it will completely ruin the weekend.

Now, I don't want you to feel like I'm turning you into some sort of Stepford girlfriend:

> *I can't complain about anything on the first date. I can only talk about happy topics. And now, months later, you're telling me that once again I can't complain on our first weekend away. At what point has "being nice" become "being obedient"?*

This is a very important point, so let me explain. On both the first date and this first romantic weekend away, I'm trying to encourage you to put your best foot forward. I don't want to lobotomize you into some happy airhead. And if you ever feel like your boyfriend doesn't value your intelligence, you need to have a conversation about that *immediately*. And if he's not interested in talking about it, then you have to break up with him *immediately*.

There are moments in a relationship, though, where it isn't all about brutal honesty. If you just found out that your grandmother passed away, it isn't the best time for your boyfriend to tell you that he thinks you're messy. You see what I mean? As long as you feel like you're in a relationship where you *could* spill your guts at any time, it's okay to admit that some moments are better than others for actually doing it.

Now, let's go back to the hotel room. There actually are some exceptions to my rule of not saying anything bad about the accommodations:

Moments When You CAN
Object to the Hotel Room

Moment #1: You're in a bad room at a nice hotel. If your boyfriend picked a place that isn't super-fancy, there's no point in saying that you wish the sheets were softer because all the rooms will have the same sheets. On the flip side, though, if you're in a nice place and you get assigned to a room with a bad smell, you can and should absolutely see if there's another room available.

Moment #2: He doesn't like the place and wants to know what you think. If it's clear that he's not satisfied and wants to switch rooms (or hotels), then you should absolutely chime in. If you like the place, he'll then feel like it's okay to stay. And if you don't like it, he knows to make a switch because there's no reason for you both to be unhappy.

Moment #3: There's just something about the room you can't live with. Everyone's got a parachute cord, and sometimes you just have to pull it. When you arrive at your "rustic" room and see a raccoon on the bed, you may have to push the panic button. Could he be annoyed? Yes. Is that better than you living in fear of a raccoon all weekend? Yes.

Once the trip is over, it's a lot easier to give feedback. Let's say your boyfriend picked a place that was perfectly nice but just not your style. If your taste in hotels and his taste in hotels don't seem to be in sync, you should have a conversation about that. You don't have to have it *during* the first trip, because he won't be able to relax for the rest of the weekend. But if he took you to a bed and breakfast, and you prefer not to sleep in a house of complete strangers, he needs to know that. You can tell him a few days after the trip ends or just bring up the next time you're making plans to go away.

Not What You're After

I'd be concerned about guys who are super-enthusiastic about going away with you when the topic comes up in conversation . . . and then never do a damn thing about it. It's not a good sign if you have to constantly remind your boyfriend about the idea. You'll probably try to convince yourself that everything's okay:

> *He probably just doesn't have the money right now, and that's why he's reluctant to bring up the topic of a weekend away.*

That's nonsense, and you know it. Even if there are financial constraints, a guy who is serious about you will leap at the idea of going away somewhere together. There are ways of doing a romantic weekend without spending a lot of money. You could borrow a friend's apartment in another city. You can wait until there's a great deal on the Internet. You can go somewhere off season. The point is, there's always a way to make it work. It's not about how much you spend; it's about being together.

The same thing holds true about time constraints. If he's having a crazy patch at work, he can ask you to help with the planning by making reservations. But just because he's busy doesn't mean everything else should grind to a halt. He's always going to be busy, but if he's into the relationship, he'll find a way to make a romantic weekend away happen.

Let Him Down Easy

Do not go on a romantic weekend trip with a guy if you know you're going to break up with him when you get back. It's as simple as that. Women tell me things like, "He wanted to take me to Vegas and I had never been. So how could I say no?" Well, sorry, ladies, that's just not good enough.

You're setting yourself up for a terrible weekend and a terrible reputation when you return. And the next woman he dates may never get the chance to go to Vegas, since you've put a bad taste in his mouth about that city.

Remember: The goal isn't to suck as much money out of him as possible before you break up. Instead, it's more important to act with class even during the toughest moments of the relationship.

CHAPTER 10

Even Men Need Hugs (Sometimes)

When One of You Has a Bad Week

A true sign of a healthy and stable relationship is when the two of you want to be around each other during a bad day. Back in Chapter Four, when I was discussing conversation topics for the first date, I told you to keep things upbeat. But, look, we all know that every day isn't magical. Now's the time to take off the candy coating.

Let's first talk about what guys are looking for when they go through a rough patch. By "rough patch," I'm talking about those days we all have where our jobs, our families, or just the world in general is driving us nuts:

- ♥ You messed up something important at work and now your boss is pissed off at you.
- ♥ Your sink is stopped up (again), and so your bathroom has become a biohazard.
- ♥ On your way to work, you spill coffee on: your new outfit, your hand (burning the skin), the person next to you on the subway, and that person's tiny dog.
- ♥ Your mom was nagging you about the fact that you can't come home for Aunt Linda's forty-seventh birthday (even

though it's on a Wednesday night, you have a full-time job, and since when did a forty-seventh birthday become a milestone?).

♥ Someone rear-ended you and as you were getting out of the car to inspect the damage, you twisted an ankle. Oh, and your car insurance company blows and won't pay for anything.

When these moments hit—and they hit all of us sooner or later—most women think that guys want to be alone. Either that, or they want some sort of sexual favor to cheer them up. But let's be serious. You're not in high school anymore.

In reality, here's what mature guys want you to do:

♥ Listen to them explain the problem. Oftentimes, simply talking about things out loud will make him feel better. So let him speak. And if he rambles on for a bit, don't look bored.

> "If I'm having a terrible week at work, the best thing my girlfriend can do to help is just listen and be supportive."
> —Carl, Denver, CO

♥ Be discreet. Don't discuss his problems with your friends or family unless he gives you the okay to do so. The last thing he wants is to have one of your friends tell him that they're sorry he lost the big account at work. All he will be thinking is, "How the hell does she know about that?!"

♥ Plan a diversion. This doesn't have to be sex! A movie, pizza night, even a trip to the mall—these all help him focus on the positive.

> *"The best thing you can say is 'let me take you somewhere to help you get your mind off work.'"*
>
> —Bill, Atlanta, GA

♥ If possible, offer some potential solutions. You don't have to have the same job as him to understand that an overly demanding boss is a pain in the neck. Most of your life experiences will offer helpful insight into what he's dealing with. And even if you don't have the magic solution, you're trying, and that means the world to him.

However, the single biggest thing men are looking for when they're having a bad day is something you can definitely give him:

♥ A little love and a little understanding. It's the simplest solution, and it's always the best. Your boyfriend is feeling frustrated, so now probably isn't the best time to point out all of his flaws. If he's in a fight with his boss, don't tell him it's because he hasn't been working hard enough. Take his side for a day or two and then you can give him a nudge in the right direction.

If you're not sure which of these tips is most appropriate for the situation your boyfriend is in, *then just ask him.* If you say, point blank, "How can I help?" he'll reply with something simple like, "Let's go get a burger together." The truth is that in a good relationship, merely having you around makes things better.

The Shoe on the Other Foot

Obviously, your boyfriend is not the only one who's going to have bad days. Some days, your number will come up. Now, the guy's point of view may sound like it's irrelevant here. I mean, if I were you, I'd be saying:

Um . . . Janis, who cares what he wants if I'm the one having a bad day!

The reason it's nice to talk about what your boyfriend wants when you're having a bad week is because *he's there to help.* In the past, you've always had your family or a group of friends that you turned to for advice. You can obviously still use them, but your boyfriend hopes you will feel comfortable coming to him for advice as well. Even if it's a topic on which he may not be an expert (your relationship with your sister, for example), he can still listen and rub your shoulders.

I'll tell you something: These bad days actually give you a golden opportunity to see just how strong a bond you have with your boyfriend.

Ways in Which a Bad Day Actually Helps You Gauge the Strength of Your Relationship

1. *Do you feel calmer just by having your boyfriend around?* If his presence alone makes you feel calmer on a stressful day, then you know you've got something very special.

2. *Is he there for you?* The death of your grandmother out-
    ranks poker night with his friends. So, quite simply,
    does he cancel poker night in order to be with you?

3. *Do you feel comfortable confiding in him?* You should
    open up to your boyfriend not because you have to but
    because you *want* to. If you're rushing to seek his input,
    that's a very good sign.

4. *If you do confide in him, how does he respond?* Does he tell
    you to lighten up and get over it? Or does he offer sug-
    gestions and comfort instead of turning the conversa-
    tion into a "whose life sucks more" competition?

5. *Does he make you feel bad about feeling bad?* Does he say
    things like, "This would be a lovely evening if you
    weren't complaining about your migraine headache"?
    He should be saying things like, "I'm going to make this
    a lovely evening to help your migraine go away."

6. *Do you start to feel better?* Your boyfriend may not have
    the solution to all your problems. But the strength of a
    good relationship should overcome the day-to-day speed
    bumps of life without much difficulty.

I'm not going to give an answer key as though this test were
a quiz in *Seventeen*: "If you answered yes to five or more questions, then you have the dreamiest guy ev-uh!!!!!!" Real life is
more complicated than that. Actually, that's a lie. It's more
simple. He should want to help when you're feeling glum.
And you should want to accept his help. End of story.

The Elephant in the Room

There is, of course, one possibility I haven't discussed yet. And the reason I haven't talked about it is because it can be really stressful. I'm talking about the elephant in the room:

What if the relationship is the source of the bad day?

It's an ugly possibility. But it's also a legitimate one, so we can't just shove it into a corner and not think about it again.

What do you do if the problem you're dealing with is the relationship itself? Most women think the following is the right answer:

Well, we're not married. We're just dating. So the guy figures that either the problems will just work themselves out naturally. If they don't, then we can just break up.

Look, I'll be honest. Guys aren't going to want to rush off to couples counseling just because you've hit a rough patch. (In fact, they probably won't want to do that even after you're married, but that's a subject for a different book.) But, at the same time, guys aren't morons. By this stage in the relationship, they appreciate that the two of you have something worth fighting for. He'd rather sit down and talk about the problem than say nothing and watch the relationship go up in smoke.

Needless to say, having a conversation about your relationship is easier said than done. How do you bring up the topic? And what do you say?

There's no magic answer here, ladies. I wish I could say,

"Tell him you love him and everything will be fine!" It's a little more complicated than that, unfortunately.

But it can still be done. Here are some tips that I highly recommend:

Tip #1: Sooner Rather Than Later

Whatever the problem is—he's upset because you said he was a bad kisser or you're upset because he seemed grumpy the night he met your sister—it's only going to grow worse if you let it stew. So don't postpone the conversation just because it's unpleasant. The sooner you talk, the sooner things can get better.

Tip #2: There's No Great Time, but There Are a Few Terrible Times

There's no perfect moment to have a difficult conversation about the relationship. But some moments are particularly bad. If he's running out the door to catch a plane or you're suffering from food poisoning, then the conversation can wait until later. And try not to talk as you're falling asleep at night. This conversation is beyond important and you should both be fully awake.

Tip #3: Set the Tone, and He'll Follow

If the first thing out of your mouth is, "You've been driving me up a goddamn wall lately!" then how do you think the rest of the conversation will play out? If you start instead by saying, "Something's clearly up—we should talk," then the conversation will be much more productive.

Tip #4: Once You Start the Conversation, Don't Stop

If you're sitting down to watch *American Idol* and suddenly the conversation just sort of happens, then you should talk.

Don't wait. You can go on the Internet later and see who was voted off (or buy a TiVo).

Tip #5: Not Everything Has to Be Resolved Immediately

Sometimes, the problem is a simple misunderstanding that's quickly resolved with a chat. For example, you were annoyed that he keeps taking you out for Indian food because you told him on the first date you hate Indian food. It turns out that he simply missed that comment entirely, and now that he knows, he's embarrassed and promises to make it up to you.

But sometimes it's not that easy. Maybe you're offended by the behavior of one his friends, but your boyfriend doesn't want to cut off contact with someone he's known for fifteen years. The point to remember is that you don't have to resolve everything during the first conversation. It's okay to stop and take a breather for a while. Getting the ball rolling gives you a chance to get the problem to be solved eventually.

Tip #6: End the Conversation on an Optimistic Note

If the topic you were discussing was something truly disastrous—he's sleeping with someone else—then you need to break up. But if it's something that can be worked out over time, having a little optimism goes a long way. If you make the last thing you say, "I know we can figure this out," it increases the chances of that actually happening.

Remember: If something really is wrong, then your boyfriend *wants* to have this conversation. He doesn't just want to throw the whole relationship away. Even if the conversation is difficult, he won't be frustrated at you for bringing it up in the first place.

One Final Note

Relationships can be stressful. But sometimes the relationship can just be a scapegoat:

> SOMETIMES THERE'S SOMETHING OUTSIDE THE
> RELATIONSHIP THAT'S BOTHERING YOU BUT YOU TAKE
> YOUR FRUSTRATION OUT ON EACH OTHER.

For the record, when I say "taking your frustration out," I don't mean scary behavior like throwing vases around the living room and yelling F-bombs every three minutes. If your boyfriend is doing that, he has some anger management issues that need to be worked out, pronto.

What I'm talking about is the more common, but still annoying, behavior. Have you ever:

♥ Inexplicably gotten mad at your boyfriend for doing something annoying, even though he's done it a hundred times before and it's never bothered you?
♥ Shot down his social plans without any explanation?
♥ Pretended as though you were listening to what he was saying, but, in fact, all you were really doing was nodding and saying, "Fine, whatever"?
♥ Criticized his apartment, hairstyle, or friends for no apparent reason?
♥ Said something like, "You can be a real jackass sometimes!"?

If the two of you are having a problem with your relationship, that's one thing. But guys hate when a work problem suddenly results in a meaningless argument with them. We all take our frustrations out on the ones we're closest to, but DO NOT ABUSE THAT PRIVILEGE.

He'll give you some leeway here because he loves you, but sooner or later the rope is going to snap. If your guy can't help make things better, don't assume he's part of the problem.

Not What You're After

Be careful about guys who suddenly become condescending when times get tough for him. This behavior drives me CRAZY! But I get even more upset when I hear about women who put up with it and blame themselves for his tough week at work. Don't ever give up your dignity and self-respect like that.

Look, your boyfriend can be cranky. That happens. No problem. But if he suddenly decides that you're not going to be able to help him with his "big boy problems," then warning bells should sound all over the place. You may not understand everything about his job (and vice versa, by the way), but you certainly understand enough to be useful. And he should never belittle you, no matter what the situation.

Bottom line: If he doesn't find you helpful, then why are you with him?

Let Him Down Easy

Do not throw painful moments back in your boyfriend's face if you decide to part ways. In the heat of the moment, it can be tempting to say something like, "A real man wouldn't have whined when he didn't get the promotion. A real man would have gotten the promotion in the first place!"

You're classier than that. You helped him through a bad week, and that's something he'll always appreciate. Don't destroy all the good things you did in a relationship just because you realize you're not going to marry each other.

I always say, "Don't burn the bridge, because you might be standing on it."

CHAPTER 11

There's No Such Thing as Too Many Electronic Gadgets

Birthdays, Valentine's Day, and Other Special Occasions

The longer you're together, the more special occasions you'll have. And the better these special occasions go, the longer you'll be together. Get the idea?

Let's start with the most basic of all celebrations: the birthday. When his birthday comes around, the most important thing to remember is:

> HE DOES **NOT** WANT A SURPRISE PARTY.

Guys are control freaks, and when there's a surprise party, they don't get to be in control. A surprise party is something they (may) trust to their mother, their best friend from childhood, or, eventually, their wife. But, as of now, you're none of those things.

If you're together forever, there will be plenty of birthdays when you can throw him a surprise. But there is NOTHING worse than being at a surprise party for someone who doesn't want it. Awkward!

Now, that said, guys do want you to plan *something* for their birthday . . . just discuss it with them ahead of time. On basically every other occasion—anniversaries, Valentine's Day, your birthday—the guy tends to take the lead on the event planning. So it will be a nice treat for him if you take the reins on his birthday.

So what does he want to do? Well, I've got news for you: He doesn't need a fancy celebration to be happy.

Nice and Simple Ways to Celebrate Your Boyfriend's Birthday

Activity	Just Remember That
Romantic dinner out just the two of you.	You should pay. (It's HIS birthday.)
A small dinner party with friends.	"Small" means less than ten people.
Go see a sporting event.	Try not to act bored out of your mind, even if you are. Hey— maybe you'll get one of those free T-shirts they shoot into the stands during time-outs!
Go see a live show of his favorite band.	Just because you like the Dixie Chicks doesn't mean he does.

Whatever activity you do, be sure you also get him a gift. Even if he says he doesn't want anything, he's lying. *Everyone* likes getting presents on their birthday. No man is too macho for that!

"Presents? I love presents! Did I say I love presents? Because I do—large and small."

—Roger, Baltimore, MD

When the subject of birthday presents comes up, I always get the following question from women:

Is he expecting a blow job as a birthday present?

The question is a little vulgar, but admit that you've wondered about it! Here's the deal: Obviously, every guy loves sex, and he certainly won't be disappointed if he gets some on his birthday. But here are two things to keep in mind:

1. You still have to get him a real gift that you can wrap.

2. Guys hope that sex isn't just a special occasion event. It should be a natural part of your relationship, not just something that happens on birthdays. He'd rather you guys have an active, enjoyable sex life than get laid on his birthday . . . and then not again for months.

Since sex doesn't really count as a gift, what else should you get him? Well, it obviously depends on how long you guys have been together. A guy you've been seeing for two years deserves a nicer gift than a guy you've been seeing for two months.

If you've only been together for a little bit, here are some simple ideas that always work well:

♥ Books. Books can be a bit impersonal unless you put a little thought into it. The best-case scenario is where you get him a book you've already read that you think he'll really enjoy. (And, by the way, get him a new copy. Don't just rewrap the one you already own. Then it's not a gift—it's a loan.)

♥ Bottle of Scotch (or other fancy spirit). A bottle of wine is too impersonal—that's what you bring as a hostess gift to a dinner party. And beer is too cheap. But if he drinks hard liquor, a bottle of his favorite brand is always appreciated, because it shows that you've been paying attention to his individual tastes. If you want to mix it up, you can get him a different brand from his usual libation, but be sure you're going up the price ladder, not down. A guy will try any booze that's more expensive and fancy than his usual drink. But if you're going to get him the cheap stuff, you might as well not even bother.

♥ Bar accessories. Stylish and cool. Martini glasses, fancy wine opener, beer steins—all of these will be welcome gifts.

Personally, I'd stay away from gift certificates. They're too impersonal, even for a guy you've just started dating. And don't give him any decorations for his home—it's too much too soon.

Now, if you've been together for many months, here are some additional gift ideas you can consider:

♥ Clothes. For men, clothes are a bit more personal than a bottle of wine, which is why I think it's best to wait to give him a shirt until you've been together for a bit. Just make sure you give him something he'll actually wear, not something you wish he would wear.

♥ Clothing accessories. These gifts are just as chic as clothes and oftentimes less expensive. Wallets, hats, scarves, sunglasses, shoes, and belts are all nice options.

And if you've been together over a year, here are a few extra ideas:

♥ Any electronic device that he doesn't already have. Electronic gadgets always get men excited. (Just be sure you keep the receipt.)

♥ Cologne. Only do this if he already wears cologne. If he doesn't, this gift says, "Um . . . you smell."

♥ Art. This is a gift that only works if you really know his taste. How you decorate your home is a very personal thing—even for men—and if he isn't crazy about the art you just gave him, he has a dilemma: He can either look at a piece of art he doesn't like or offend you. So if you're not a 100 percent sure, I'd recommend something else.

♥ Jewelry. No, you don't have to get him a man-diamond. But a watch is a very sophisticated gift that every guy will love.

Happy Birthday to You

When it comes to your birthday, you'll obviously know how you'll want to celebrate it. But your boyfriend may not. So guys really love it when you give them a hint as to what you want to do. He already knows he should get you a gift, but he won't know if you want to have an intimate night or a big party on your birthday unless you tell him.

Now, when I tell women that piece of advice, there's usually the following concern:

Well, Janis, what if he doesn't ask what I want to do on my birthday? If I just sort of bring up the topic out of the blue, isn't that a little self-centered?

Look, in a perfect world, he'll know your birthday is coming up and ask you what you want to do. But sometimes that doesn't happen. So you definitely have a green light to start discussing what you want to do about two to three weeks ahead of time. He'll think you're being organized, not self-centered.

The key is *how* you bring up the topic of your birthday. Your boyfriend will think you're a whackadoodle if you tell him a month into the relationship, "On my birthday, ten months from now, I want you to throw me a party at a fancy restaurant for twenty of my friends."

Instead, you'll get much better results if you say something like this: "My birthday is next week and I was thinking of throwing a little dinner party with about six friends. What do you think? Want to help me with the menu?"

There are, however, a few special situations where it gets confusing:

Special Birthday Situation #1: Your Birthday Arrives Very Soon After You and Your Boyfriend Start Dating

In this situation, your boyfriend isn't responsible for planning the birthday party. He should come, but you (or your friends) should be the one running the show.

Special Birthday Situation #2: Milestone Birthday

Let's say that during your first year of dating, you have your thirtieth birthday. It's a milestone. So is it weird if all your boyfriend wants to do is take you to dinner? I mean, he'd do that even if it was your twenty-eighth birthday, so shouldn't he do something extra-special for your thirtieth?

No. Be realistic. If you've only been together for a few months, he isn't going to buy you diamond earrings and throw you a gigantic party just because you're turning thirty. If you have a milestone birthday during the first year of dating, you can expect a really nice present from your boyfriend, but not a Donald Trump—style blowout bash. You can throw that party for yourself, but it isn't your boyfriend's responsibility to do it for you.

Special Birthday Situation #3: Your Birthdays Are Near Each Other

If that's the case, don't insist on having a joint party. It's still too early in the relationship for that. You should each have your own event (and try to make them different). If you go out for sushi for one person's birthday, maybe stay in and cook for the second person's. Or go out for Italian food instead of Japanese food. Or at least try a different sushi restaurant!

Roses Are Red

When it comes to the topic of Valentine's Day, every woman I talk to says the same thing:

Men secretly hate Valentine's Day, right? In their view, they don't need a holiday to show their love.

Well, here's the thing. I surveyed a bunch of my clients and asked them that very question. Here's how I put the question:

When you have a girlfriend, is Valentine Day's a fun celebration or a pain in the neck?

Now here's the amazing result. *Every guy I asked said it was a fun celebration.* That's right—every one! So despite what you think, men really enjoy the holiday. And to make sure you both enjoy it as much as possible, here's my advice:

Janis's Five Steps to a Great Valentine's Day

1. Don't describe anything your boyfriend does on Valentine's Day as "cheesy." It will hurt his feelings and, as a result, next year he may not do anything at all.

2. You can be a little annoyed if he doesn't get you flowers. But you *can't* be annoyed with the type of flowers he does get you.

3. If you don't like chocolates, tell him ahead of time.

4. Don't start making Valentine's Day plans until February 1st. If you start talking about in November, you're
   going to scare him.

5. If he buys you dinner and gets you flowers, don't expect
   an overly fancy gift. He's already spending a lot, and
   the gift will be something simple but sweet.

And the most important tip of all:

6. Don't forget that it's a joint holiday.

He's your Valentine too. He'll shower you with flowers and
love, but he'd love just a little something in return. Translation:
Be sure you get him a gift too (but it doesn't have to be flowers!).

It's a Seven-and-a-Half-Month
Celebration!

And now the most confusing celebration of them all: the
anniversary. Why is the anniversary confusing?

1. Men don't like to celebrate anniversaries until they're
   married.

2. No one can ever agree when you started dating.

Let's start with the first reason. This sounds like I'm giving
men a bad reputation here, but I'm not. In the minds of most
guys, the anniversary is an occasion where you celebrate the
date of your marriage. And since you're not married, what is
there to celebrate?

Let me put it in a different way: Do you celebrate Bastille Day? Unless your grandfather was born in Marseilles, I'm guessing the answer is no, because it's only a holiday in France. If you move to France, you'll start celebrating it, but until then, it's not a holiday for you.

Men apply the same logic to anniversaries—when they're married, they can't wait to celebrate them. But until then, it's not a holiday for them.

Okay—I'm being a bit extreme, I know. Most guys could easily be convinced to celebrate a dating anniversary because any excuse to drink champagne is worthwhile!

The problem, as I said above, is that there always seems to be disagreements over when you started dating. When do you celebrate your anniversary if you're dating but not yet married? Is it:

♥ The day you met?
♥ The first date?
♥ The day you first kissed?
♥ The day you went exclusive?
♥ The day you first had sex?
♥ The day you just felt like you were a couple?

There's no correct answer. And as the two of you debate what to do, the anniversary suddenly seems less celebratory and much more stressful. So guys would just prefer to wait until after they're married to celebrate an anniversary because then everyone can agree on a date.

Just to throw another wrench into the works, there's also this issue:

> GUYS DON'T WANT TO OBSERVE
> TWELVE DIFFERENT ANNIVERSARIES A YEAR.

For men, your anniversary should be an annual event. Here's what they *don't* want to celebrate:

Dating Anniversaries That Men DON'T Want to Celebrate

👎 Six weeks together!
👎 Four months since our first kiss!
👎 The tenth date!
👎 Seven-and-a-half months since we met!
👎 The one year anniversary of our third date!

For guys, celebrating a five-month anniversary is pointless—it only waters down the significance of your actual anniversary.

Now, if you're thinking:

Janis, I get what you're saying, but celebrating an anniversary is just really important to me!

Then I have a solution for you:

1. Just pick a date that's generally close to your first date and agree that's your dating anniversary.

2. Once you pick that anniversary date, stick to it. No more debating about when your anniversary is!

3. Do NOT celebrate any other anniversaries. One per year.

4. If you do get married someday, your wedding day is your new anniversary.

Not What You're After

I'd be very skeptical about a guy who refuses to celebrate Valentine's Day, and uses the "It's a Hallmark holiday" line as an excuse. God, that drives me crazy. He's right, of course—it is a Hallmark holiday. But who cares? Mother's Day is also a Hallmark holiday, so are you suddenly not going to call your mom on the second Sunday in May?

A holiday can be commercialized but still have a sweet sentiment. A good boyfriend should have already realized this. He doesn't need to talk about what's wrong with every holiday—he should focus on what's good about it. Your boyfriend can give you flowers on Valentine's Day without being a sellout. If he complains through every holiday, tell him he needs to get a grip or get a new girlfriend.

Let Him Down Easy

Here's one of the supposedly unwritten rules of dating:

> YOU CAN'T BREAK UP WITH SOMEONE
> RIGHT BEFORE A HOLIDAY.

I don't like this rule because it's really a case-by-case scenario. On one hand, you think: There's never a good time to break up with someone, so you should just do it and get it over with. How can you celebrate Valentine's Day if you know you're going to dump your boyfriend the following week?

On the other hand, it seems beyond harsh to dump someone before a big holiday. I mean, if you break up with him the day before Valentine's Day, aren't you pretty much ruining that holiday for him forever?

My advice is that you should plan ahead. You don't just wake up one morning and say, "I'm done!" It's a decision you think about over the course of a few weeks. So if you're having doubts in January, set a goal of trying to decide what you want to do by February 1st. If you can't come to a decision, that's okay. But then you should take a few more weeks to decide.

If it's crystal clear on February 13th that you want to dump him, it was probably crystal clear two weeks earlier, so why not just do it then?

CHAPTER 12

He's Just as Nervous as You Are

Meeting Each Other's Families

For most couples, meeting each other's parents is the most stressful time of the entire relationship. The first date, the first fight, moving in together—these moments all pale in comparison to the anxiety felt when you bring your sweetheart home for a family BBQ.

The first, and most obvious, question that arises is:

When should we meet each other's families?

Guys prefer to meet the parents when it's clear to them that the two of you will be together for a while. Most of my clients tell me this translates to around *three months*. That's not a hard and fast rule, but the idea is that they DON'T want to do it after three dates, when it's not yet clear if you guys are really an item.

Now, when women hear this "three month rule" the first thing they try to do is tell me about the special circumstances:

Well, Janis, what if my parents happen to be in town for a visit? Am I actually supposed to tell my parents, "I have a new guy, but you can't meet him yet?"

Yes. That's *exactly* what you tell your parents. Needless to say, some guys may be okay meeting your parents that soon. But most guys would rather wait, and you really shouldn't hold that against them.

If you guys stick together for a while you'll spend PLENTY of time with your parents, so don't worry if it doesn't happen on this trip.

> "I want to meet her family when it becomes a serious relationship."
>
> —Andy, Washington, D.C.

"We've Heard a Lot About You!"

When the time does finally arrive for him to meet your parents, it's helpful if it happens on your turf. If your parents come to visit you guys, that's much less intense than if you go to stay with your parents.

If your parents live close to you, then it's fine to go to their place . . . because after a few hours you can leave! I'm not insulting your parents. But let me tell you one thing: Your boyfriend wants the first meeting with your parents to last a few hours, not a few days. That's why a vacation with your family isn't the best way to start things off. It's overwhelming.

If you are, in fact, able to arrange it so that your parents come visit you, don't require your boyfriend to be with them twenty-four hours a day. You've got to ease him in.

Besides pacing yourself on the schedule, here are a few other things guys are hoping you'll do to make the meeting go as well as possible:

1. Be calm and be relaxed. Remember: He's been down this road before. He's met other people's parents. And some of those parents were really crazy. So he's prepared for anything. But if you're happy and calm about the occasion, it makes it so much easier for him to be as well.

2. Schedule an event that doesn't last forever. Make the first meeting over a meal, if you can, because that gives a nice sense of structure to the occasion. It's way too open ended if you say, "Come spend Saturday with me and my parents." Your boyfriend won't be sure when he can leave without being insulting to your parents. As a result, he'll probably wind up spending all day with you guys, and then he'll feel overloaded.

3. Warn him about your dad. Here's the thing about dads: They can be *very* protective of their little girls. Dads can be very rude or aggressive without meaning to be. Now, you may not think your dad is scary, but he can put on a different persona when he's meeting some dude who wants to shack up with his precious angel. Know what I mean?

As a result, guys want to know ahead of time what they can expect from your dad. It's important to your boyfriend that he has the respect of your father. Before he walks into the job interview, it's helpful to know what the boss is looking for.

If you're not quite sure how to describe your dad to your boyfriend, this chart will help:

Type of Dad	How He's Likely to Behave Around Your Boyfriend
The General	Orders him around and instills a sense of fear and intimidation.
The Interviewer	Asks him a minimum of thirty-seven questions per hour.
The Silent type	Stares at your boyfriend throughout the entire meal but says nothing. (Note: Your boyfriend will be scared to death.)
The Reminiscer	Sings the praises of your ex-boyfriends.
The Know It All	Tells your boyfriend lots of facts about the world (many of which are untrue).
The Competitor	Compare your boyfriend's career to his own.

4. Tell your parents not to talk about marriage or children. Comments about marriage and children will totally blindside and annoy your boyfriend. Men know that your parents want grandkids ASAP because *all parents* want that. And while it's fine for your parents to apply marriage pressure after a while, it's weird if they jump to that topic during the first meeting. It makes it seem like they're less interested in him as a person and more interested in him as a reproductive machine. Now, I know what you're thinking:

Look, Janis, my parents are crazy! I can't control everything they say!

I hear you. The good news: Your boyfriend knows you can't control everything your parents do. So all he asks is that if your parents are crazy, give them a friendly call before the meeting and remind them not to ask about the wedding guest list because, hello, you're not even engaged yet. And if your parents do slip up, try to steer the conversation elsewhere. And then, later on, tell your boyfriend you're sorry. It's not your fault, but sometimes you have to clean up after other people's messes.

Only Halfway There

Once you've successfully introduced your boyfriend to your mom and dad, you now have to meet his parents. Don't worry—it's going to be easy. It's almost always tougher for him to meet your family than the other way around because, like it or not, parents tend to be a bit more protective of their daughters. As progressive as we've all become, there's still an element of "go get 'em, tiger!" that many fathers apply to their sons. With their daughters, though, dads tend to think, "If the guy you're dating isn't good enough, I'll tell him!"

Your boyfriend's parents are going to like you because you make their son happy. That said, your boyfriend still wants you to be on your best behavior when you meet his mom and dad. Here what that means:

1. Be polite. No woman ever thinks this will be a problem:

Janis—give me a break! I'll be the most respectful person his parents have ever met!

Well, you say that. And you probably mean it. And then, somehow, you wind up in a heated argument with his dad about politics. And that's followed by an awkward debate with his mother about whether married women should change their last names. Yes, you should stand up for what you believe, and if you become part of the family, there will be many years during which you can debate his parents. But be diplomatic the first time around.

2. Don't get trapped by their questions. Sometimes it's hard to be diplomatic because his parents start asking you crazy questions that totally throw you off your game:

Weirdly Personal Questions That His Parents May Ask You During the First Meeting

♥ Do you plan to quit your job when you have children?
♥ How many people have you dated seriously before our son?
♥ Was the college that you went to your first choice?
♥ Are your parents planning to pay for a wedding?
♥ I'm sure your family's Thanksgiving traditions are nice, but Ted's never missed the holiday dinner at our home, and you wouldn't want him to start now, would you?

The trick for you is to employ a little bit of political savvy; answer the question without really answering it. For example:

His mom: Where are you guys spending Christmas this year?

Your boyfriend: We haven't really dealt with that yet, Mom.

His mom [*to you*]:   Why don't you come to our house this year?

You: That's a very sweet offer, thank you.

Your boyfriend: Mom, like I said, we haven't talked about it.

His mom: Well, that's why we're talking about it now. [*To you*] What do you say? Christmas in Chicago sound good?

You: It does sound great. But before Jim and I commit to anything, I think we'll need talk it over.

Obviously, this is just an example, but it shows how you can be polite without locking yourself in. If you say you're going to their place for Christmas, you're trapped. His parents will consider it a done deal, because they're excited to spend time with you guys. Your parents will then get upset that you're not going to their place for Christmas, and you're pretty much screwed.

3. Don't make fun of his mother. Obviously, you're smart enough not to say anything insulting *during* the meeting (I hope!). Thankfully I *don't* have a story to tell here—because if I did it would be a cringe fest.

But you should still avoid making fun of his mother the minute you get into the car to drive home. Even if your boyfriend has made sarcastic remarks about his mom in the past, he still loves her and needs you to do the same. You've got to love before you can mock. Once it's clear to him that you love his mother too, then you can both make fun of her outfit that looks like it was bought in 1987 (nice shoulder pads, lady!).

4. Don't completely blame him if his parents are nuts.
Your boyfriend didn't pick his parents . . . just like you didn't pick yours. What else can you say?

5. Show his sister some love. If your boyfriend has a sister, she is going to be very excited about having you around. If she's the only daughter, I can guarantee that she has always wanted a sister of her own. Now, I don't mean to jump the gun. I know you're not married. Your boyfriend's sister isn't *your* sister (yet). But try to treat her like a sister. It will impress everyone in his family. So if your boyfriend's younger sister asks you to come up to her room to give her some dating advice, say yes—because her brothers always say no (and then fart in her room).

Not What You're After

Ladies, I'd be skeptical about guys who are mean to their own mother. This is an old adage, and it's absolutely true. Obviously, your boyfriend and his mom can have disagreements. But there's a big difference between him making an annoyed remark and insulting his own mother:

Annoyed Remark (Okay)	Insult (Troubling)
"Mom, stop nagging me about when I'm going to get a new carpet for my living room."	"Mom, you have terrible taste."
"Mom, I already told you I can't have dinner next Friday because I'll be out of town."	"Mom, when it comes to dates and times you're a total moron. Seriously."

"Mom, I do wear the sweater you got me for Christmas. I'm just not wearing it right now."	"That sweater is hideous, Mom."
"I don't know why my sister isn't returning your phone calls promptly, Mom. Maybe you should ask her."	"Um, hello? She isn't calling you back because you drive her goddamn crazy, Mom. Can't you see that?"
"I know you only want to help, but, trust me, this isn't the right time to ask my boss for a raise."	"A former receptionist is telling me how to be a businessman?"

It's fine if he complains about his parents in private. But when you're with them, they deserve some basic respect, no matter how crazy they are.

If a guy doesn't love his own mother, it makes you wonder how he'll be feeling about you in twenty years.

And, for the record, I'd also question any guy who is reluctant to meet your parents, especially if you've met his. It's similar to the issue of wanting to meet your friends: These are important people in your life, and if your boyfriend isn't interested in them, it means he's not interested enough in you. And what do we do with guys who aren't interested enough in us? We cut bait and move on!

Let Him Down Easy

Sometimes you like a guy, but his family is completely WACKO. In a perfect world, you don't want that to influence your feelings about your boyfriend, but we all know it does. You can't help but wonder if the apple doesn't fall far from the tree. Does your boyfriend have the crazy gene?

Even if your boyfriend seems fine, if you can't stand his family, that's a problem. These people are going to be at every important event in your life from now on. That can be really scary.

But here's my request: Even if his wacko family makes you want to break up with your boyfriend, don't tell him that's the only reason. It's not fair to him because there's nothing he can really do about it. Besides, there are always other reasons.

Most people have issues with their in-laws. But if you love your spouse enough, you'll put up with them. So if you can't put up with them, there must be other factors at work as well. Talk about these other reasons when you break up. Don't just tell him all the horror stories about his family (that's what nights out with your friends are for!).

Part Four

The One

CHAPTER 13

Can You Love Him as Much as Your Poodle?

Moving in Together

When it comes to living together, the question I get all the time from women is:

Do you think it's okay to move in with my boyfriend if we're not engaged yet?

Now, my response to this question is going to seem a little old-fashioned. For me, the answer is no. I don't like to see a woman move in with her boyfriend until she has an engagement ring on her finger. You know why? The minute you move in, you're going to slow down his desire to get engaged. Why would he pay for an engagement ring if you're giving him everything he wants for free? Your boyfriend now has the woman he loves living with him. His life is perfect. So why get married?

Now, I know what you're thinking:

Janis, you're really selling men short, here. I mean, sometimes a guy just wants to be sure he's a 100 percent compatible with his girlfriend before they get engaged. And living together is one final test of compatibility.

Yes, I am being a little mean to guys here. It gives me no pleasure to do it, but the evidence speaks for itself. Most of the time, when a woman lives with her boyfriend before getting engaged, it takes FOREVER to see a ring.

Now, that said, I'm realistic. I know that these days most couples start living together before they get engaged. It's such a common practice that many women feel weird not doing it, especially if the guy wants to.

So if you're feeling a lot of pressure to move in together before getting engaged, let me just say this:

> DO NOT MOVE IN TOGETHER UNLESS YOU'RE
> 99.9 PERCENT CONFIDENT HE'S PLANNING TO
> GET ENGAGED TO YOU WHEN THE TIME IS RIGHT.

Let me put it to you another way: You don't want to be moving in if you think there's a chance you'll be moving out. Get what I'm saying? Breakups are hard enough. But when you add the stress of packing up everything you own and searching for a new place to live, it's unbearable. So don't put yourself in that situation.

My clients have a mixed response as to when it's appropriate to move in together. Some men agree with me that you should wait until you're practically ready to get married. Others, though, thought it wasn't necessary.

You're probably a little confused, and I understand why:

So how can I tell if there's a 99.9 percent chance he wants to get engaged to me when the time is right?

It's all about how he reacts when the subject of living together first comes up in conversation. I recommend at least six months of dating before you have this conversation. But when the topic comes up, keep your eyes peeled for his instantaneous reaction. Those first thirty seconds of the conversation are *loaded* with information.

You'll get one of three reactions from your boyfriend:

Reaction #1

His eyes light up like a Christmas tree: good!

Reaction #2

He says he doesn't think it's a good idea at this point. This reaction is not as bad as it seems. He's just being honest. If he's not ready, then it shouldn't happen yet. That doesn't mean he won't be ready in the future; he's just not ready now.

Reaction #3

He thinks about it for a little bit and then says something like, "Yeah. Sure. Why the hell not?" That's trouble! He's probably thinking less about your feelings and more about the savings that come from splitting the power bill. Sorry to be blunt, but that's the reality.

Another test you can use is to see whether he puts any thought into *when* this should happen. If he says, "Yes!" and leaves it at that, well, frankly, it's not enough. Now that you've had the moving in together conversation, he should be putting some thought into how many months from now it's going to happen. If committing to a time frame makes him uncomfortable—look out! You should suddenly feel uncomfortable too.

Whose Place Is Home?

If you get the reaction you want from your boyfriend when you talk about living together, the next big question you should be asking yourself is:

Do I move in with him or does he move in with me?

Obviously, there are a lot of factors that go into answering this question:

- ♥ Who has more space?
- ♥ Whose neighborhood is quieter?
- ♥ Whose rent is cheaper?
- ♥ Whose location is more convenient?
- ♥ Who has parking for two cars?
- ♥ Who has a roommate?
- ♥ Who has two bathrooms?
- ♥ Who has DIRECTV?

If he's moving into your place, he wants to feel welcome. The way you do that is by making room for his stuff. Even though you have more clothes than he does, you still need to make room for his possessions. It doesn't need to be an exact fifty-fifty split. But he'd like more than 5 percent of the space. So if there are ten shelves in the bathroom, he doesn't need five, but he gets more than one.

If you're moving into his place, guys don't want you to re-decorate the minute you move in. He knows that some of his stuff will have to go, but some of it should also be allowed to stay. If he has a hideous piece of art or an easy chair that's so old it's absolutely disgusting, then talk to him about it:

You: I don't know if that easy chair fits with my set of living room furniture.

Him: I've had it forever.

You: Well, since it's sort of falling apart, maybe we could move it into a more private area—the bedroom? Maybe the office?

Him: Yeah, I guess that could work.

You: Or, better yet, we could get you a new one.

Him: I don't know. It's got sentimental value.

You: Well, maybe we can look at some new chairs and you can see how you feel then.

Him: Yeah. Okay.

Now, if he doesn't take the hint that the chair is gross and should be thrown out pronto, then you can be a little more direct about your feelings:

You: I just don't feel clean when I sit in that easy chair.

Him: I've had it forever.

You: I know. But sometimes it's out with the old and in with the new.

Him: Yeah, I guess.

You: The chair smells like old cheese.

Him: Okay. You're right.

You: Thank you.

Whatever you do, just consult with him before giving away any of his stuff. You never know, that weird sculpture on the kitchen counter may have been a gift from his nephew (who's coming to visit next week).

By the way, there's one easy solution to all these problems:

> If it's possible, move into a new place
> when you guys start living together.

I know this isn't always possible:

Janis! I own my house (or apartment)! Are you saying I have to sell it?

Of course not! If one of you owns your place, then getting a new place probably isn't possible. No problem. All I'm saying is that if you're both renting, it's really nice to make a fresh start in a new place.

Let the Games Begin

Besides not throwing away (all of) his stuff, there are a few other things you can do during the first few weeks of living together that will help you guys get off on the right foot:

♥ Consult him on decorating decisions. I'll tell you something: Men care about how the place is decorated. That may surprise you, but the truth is that everyone cares about where the couch goes and what color the bedroom walls should be painted.

Now, your boyfriend will probably be more than happy to let you take the lead on the decorating. In fact, you can usually approach him having already made the decision and just ask for his rubber stamp of approval.

But even that small amount of involvement is important. So before you paint the bedroom pink, make sure he signs off on it.

♥ Love him as much as your pet. A lot of single women have a cat, dog, or goldfish that's been with them forever. Guys know that moving in with you means moving in with Muffin the Cat as well. But—not surprisingly—most guys don't love it when their bed pillow is covered in cat hair. So even if Muffin's had the run of the place for years, it's time to lay down some new laws.

Sometimes, there can be a serious conflict with pets: allergies. If he loves you, your boyfriend will do his best to live with your pet. But if Muffin is giving your boyfriend deadly asthma, you can't blame him for announcing that you must choose between him and the cat. And if you choose cat, well, that's your choice. But good luck explaining it to your mother!

I should mention one other thing: If your boyfriend is willing to put up with Muffin, that's great. But it also means you then have to put up with his Great Dane, Thor.

♥ Men still need a little alone time. I touched on this in the chapter about romantic weekend getaways, but, obviously, it's even more important now that you guys are living together. Most guys need a few hours on their own each weekend. If he's living with you, it's a pretty good bet he *loves* being around you. So don't worry if he ducks into the other room to watch the end of a basketball game. He still loves you. He just needs a little alone time. Part of living together is knowing when your roommate needs a little space.

Of course, the hardest part of living together usually *isn't* the big stuff like decor. Instead, it's the small stuff like dirt on the carpet that can suddenly drive a wedge between the two of you.

What guys really appreciate is when you *tell them directly* if their behavior is driving you crazy. Don't take passive-aggressive actions. Here's what I'm talking about:

You Hate It When He	But Don't
Refuses to hang up his wet towel.	Stand by the wet towel with your eyes ablaze until he notices (because he probably won't, and then you'll just get more upset).
Leaves dirty dishes in the sink overnight.	Complain that all you do is wash dishes (because he'll tell you that's what a dishwasher is for).
Doesn't put out a new roll of paper towels after using up the old one.	Stand there, tapping the empty role against the palm of your hand (because he'll say, "Why don't you throw away the toilet paper roll, babe?").
Leaves a pile of dirty laundry in the corner of the bedroom.	Buy him a hamper (because he already has one; he just doesn't use it).
Leaves the toilet seat up.	Put a Post-it on the seat (because he'll take the Post-it off the seat and, without reading it, flush it down the toilet).

I have a funny story about leaving toilet seat up, which is one of the most hilarious (and annoying) adjustments for men when they move in with a woman. A client of mine named Simon had just moved in with a great woman named Kathleen. Everything was going well . . . except for the toilet seat. Kathleen had tried everything—notes, subtle hints, even putting the seat down right in front of him—and nothing worked. No matter what Kathleen did, Simon always found a way to leave the seat up.

Of course, Kathleen hadn't tried the most obvious solution. So she finally just put her arm on Simon's shoulder, looked him straight in the eyes, and said, "Someone else is in the house with you now. I'd really appreciate it if you could put the toilet seat down." Guess what? Simon never forgot again.

Now, inevitably, when I tell that story, I get this question:

But, Janis, shouldn't he just know that leaving the seat up or leaving dirty dishes in the sink is gross? Did he grow up in the wild? Do I really have to tell him to put the dishes in the dishwasher?

Yes! You really have to tell him! If you play the passive-aggressive game, he's not going to get the hint. And you'll just get annoyed. The whole thing is a silly waste of time. He'll be happy to change his ways. All you have to do is tell him how. Phrase your request nicely (at least the first time you ask!) and it should go well.

By the way, it's worth remembering that you could have some annoying habits as well. I know it sounds crazy—Me?! Annoying?! It happens. Even though you're probably MUCH neater than he is, there still may be some things you do that could drive him crazy, such as:

- ♥ Not cleaning your hair out of the shower drain.
- ♥ Usurping the bathroom sink from him when he's right in the middle of brushing his teeth.
- ♥ Bringing yourself a glass of water each night before bed and never asking if you can bring him one as well.
- ♥ Leaving 472 fashion/home magazines on the coffee table, so that there's no place to put a cup of coffee (or anything else).
- ♥ Having so many throw pillows on the bed that it takes him twenty-five minutes to find his own pillow each night.

The good news is that your boyfriend will play by the same rules that I asked you to follow. He won't be upset if you don't bring him a glass of water before bed because you've never had to do that before. So he'll ask nicely.

If his request is unreasonable, you can tell him that. But just because he's asking doesn't mean you have to have a fight. He wants to be the best roommate he can be—even if that means changing some old habits. You should be willing to do the same.

Splitting the Bill

Living together is obviously the most expensive and complex undertaking the two of you have done together as a couple. How do you split up the expenses? What is he expecting from you? What if one of you makes a TON more money than the other?

Here are the three things that every guy is expecting financially when you move in together:

1. You'll contribute. We're beyond the stage where this is a nice gesture that will make him smile. This is RE-QUIRED. Now, just like the weekend away, the split doesn't have to be right down the middle. But if you have any source of income, then you MUST give part of it to the living expenses.

   The easiest solution is to have each of you contribute the same percentage of your income. If, for example, you're each contributing 35 percent of your income to utilities/rent/mortgage/etc., then there's a nice equality to the process, even if the dollar amounts are different.

2. You'll have a sit down to determine specifics. The best way to figure out how much money each of you will contribute is to have a detailed conversation BEFORE you start living together. For many people, this is awkward, because you're not used to discussing your salary, your phone bill, and your Diet Coke expenditures with anyone else.

   But even if this conversation feels like a pain in the neck, you'll be happier later on that you've gotten these issues out of the way now. Plus, if you don't feel comfortable discussing money with each other, how will you ever feel comfortable discussing the subject of marriage when that comes up?

3. If things change, you'll be honest. This may be the toughest thing to do. After that initial conversation about who's paying for what, most couples never want to revisit the money issue again. But sometimes that Christmas bonus you were counting on doesn't come through. It shouldn't be a secret you keep from your

boyfriend. If your income winds up being lower (or higher) than you thought, you need to have another conversation about money. If you get in the habit of hiding money from each another, it encourages other forms of deception.

Dropping By the New Place

The final speed bump on the road to living together actually happens after you've moved in. The issue is socializing—specifically, who comes to hang out at your place. Remember: You have a roommate now, and he may or may not want your home to be the social center of the city.

Most women assume that men are hermits . . . at least compared to them:

Janis, I get the feeling that my boyfriend never wants to have people over. He'd rather just come home from work and have peace and quiet (and a beer).

That's wrong. In reality, the only thing guys want is *no surprises*.

If you're having people over, tell him. And I'm not just talking about dinner parties. You need to tell him about the small stuff too, including:

♥ A friend is coming by to borrow a sweater.
♥ You're hosting your book club on Tuesday.
♥ Your sister is coming over to watch a DVD.
♥ The house painter is coming by Saturday morning to discuss the stain on the ceiling.

♥ A friend is coming over to see the new place before the two of you go out for drinks.

Even though your boyfriend may not be participating in most of these events, he still wants to know that they're happening. He doesn't want to be wandering around in his boxer shorts Saturday morning when the house painter suddenly shows up. And he doesn't want to come home on a Wednesday night to unexpectedly find seven women discussing Toni Morrison.

Now, before you go crazy, let me clarify what I'm saying:

> YOU'RE NOT ASKING PERMISSION.
> YOU'RE JUST GIVING HIM A HEADS UP.

Your boyfriend won't object to your social plans unless he has a really good reason—he's invited his parents over for dinner the night you're hosting your book club, for example. Guys simply like to know what the social schedule is—even when they're not a part of it.

Needless to say, there will also be times when your boyfriend invites people over without telling you (especially during the NFL Playoffs). Make him play by the same rules. Let him know that you're not upset because he's watching football. You're upset because he didn't tell you he'd be watching football . . . with ten of his friends.

Eventually, checking with each other about social plans will become second nature. You just want to be sure that you don't break up before making it to that point. So be respectful and keep each other informed.

Not What You're After

Earlier in this chapter, I warned you about guys who seem lukewarm about the idea of moving in together but then do it anyway. Even worse are guys who have had lots of live-in girlfriends before you. A dubious track record like that means:

1. He has no concept of when it's an appropriate time in the relationship to move in together.

2. He hasn't learned from his mistakes.

3. He really wants to date surrogate mothers (hello, Oedipus!).

He's allowed one strike. Everyone makes mistakes when they're young. Lots of guys have lived with a girlfriend once and it didn't work out and the breakup was the worst several months of his life. Hopefully, he'll be a lot more cautious next time.

But if he's done this more than once, look out. You're probably next in a long line of ugly breakups.

Let Him Down Easy

Throughout this chapter I've gone to great lengths to help you avoid getting your heart broken by moving in with a guy when he's not ready to commit.

For the record, I need to remind you that it's a two-way street. That's right ladies: You can break his heart as well.

When a great guy, full of enthusiasm, suggests moving in together, it's really difficult to say no, even if you're not ready.

In that situation, though, you must be honest. It's so much less awkward to wait a few months than it is to move in and then break up. Do the right thing here. Move in with him if you're ready. And if you're not, then don't do it.

CHAPTER 14

Let's Talk in Private

When the Subject of Marriage
Comes Up in Conversation

Throughout this book, I've warned you many times about the dangers of bringing up the subject of marriage before it's the right time. Which naturally leads to this question:

Well, Janis, when is it the right time? I'm ready to talk about our long-term future. Is he?

Obviously, the answer depends on your age. But by the time you're in your thirties, I tell people that six months is a good rule of thumb. If you feel like six months is still too early, then you can wait a bit longer. But even the most snail-like of men should be willing to talk about marriage after a year of dating.

> *"One year is definitely serious and you should be able to lay out the timeline of the future."*
> —Roger, Baltimore, MD

I'm not saying you have to get engaged on day 366 of dating. But you do have the green light to discuss in detail where you both see this relationship going.

I don't want to give you a script for the conversation because by this point in the relationship you should already know how to talk to each other. If you're not comfortable having a serious conversation with your boyfriend, then he's not going to become your future husband. End of story.

That said, here are a few things to keep in mind when you launch into a "future of the relationship" conversation:

♥ Talk in private. A dinner party, a family reunion, a crowded airplane—these are all bad places to discuss something as private as getting married. A restaurant is okay, as long as it's not one of those French bistros where you're three inches from the next table.

♥ Don't try to have the talk as he is falling asleep. I know that it's convenient to talk at night because you're both home. But there's no reason you can't bring up the conversation during dinner or the following morning or anytime before his head is hitting the pillow.

♥ No ultimatums. The tone of the conversation is important. Guys want you to be honest, but they don't want that honesty to come across as an ultimatum. Telling him that you're basically willing and ready to get married is great news. But if you say, "I want to be engaged by Christmas," you sound less like you're confessing your love and more like you're giving him ransom demands.

The fabulous news is that once the conversation begins, your boyfriend will be excited to talk. Lots of times he'll even bring up the topic himself. Seriously! Remember: There's something great going on between the two of you. He's aware of it and he's just as excited as you are.

So What Is Your Future Together?

After you discuss the future of your relationship, you don't need to keep harping on the subject. But, at the same time, it's okay to want to see some progress. Which leaves you with a bit of a problem: When can you bring up the subject of marriage again? Well, it depends on his initial reaction:

He says something like:	"I love you and I don't see this relationship ever ending."
You should:	Do nothing for about three months. Odds are high that he's planning the perfect engagement and wants it to be a surprise. If there's no ring after three months, then you can bring up the subject of marriage again.
He says something like:	"You're wonderful. I just need a little bit more time before I'm ready to get married."
You should:	Give him about six more months. If he hasn't moved closer to marriage at that point, let him know that you're not going to wait forever.
He says something like:	"Marriage isn't something I'm really thinking about at this point."

You should:	Decide how long you're willing to wait for him: three months, six months, a year, several years . . . or not at all. And return his honesty with some of your own. Tell him, "Well . . . let's revisit the topic after the holidays. But it's something I want to discuss."

He says something like:	"I just don't see us getting married."
You should:	Say adios. Seriously—you've invested a lot, but if he tells you the relationship is never going to go where you want it to, you need to move on.

Actually, there's one more response you may get, but I saved it for last because it's my favorite!

He says something like:	"I'm ready. You're the woman I want to be with forever."

This is obviously the best response (assuming you feel the same way). The first thing you should do is kiss him! But that's just the tip of the iceberg.

When your boyfriend tells you that he's essentially ready to get married to you, here's what he hopes happens next:

Step #1: Radio Silence

Even though he basically just said that you'll be engaged soon, you're not engaged *yet*. So don't tell people that you are. The conversation you've just had with your boyfriend is very private and should remain that way for now.

Step #2: Don't Plan the Wedding Yet

This is an extension of Step #1. *You're not engaged yet! There's no wedding to plan!* I know, I know, here's what you're thinking:

> *Look, Janis, I can't help it if wedding-related ideas enter my head. I'm just so excited!*

That's totally understandable. But you've got to keep those ideas in your head. Guys don't like to put the cart before the horse. Even if getting the ring seems like a formality, enjoy it. Relish the moment! It's one of those signature events in your life. Don't skip over it just because you want to get a headstart with the florist.

Step #3: Discuss the Ring

The moment you've been waiting for! Getting an engagement ring is going to be an absolutely incredible moment in *both* of your lives.

Now, your first reaction is going to be to tell him exactly what type of ring you want. After all, you're the one who's going to be wearing it—shouldn't you have some input?

Hold your horses.

Maybe he's already bought the ring. Maybe he has a family stone that's already been bequeathed to him. Or maybe he just wants the engagement to be a total surprise because there is a certain magic that comes from doing it that way.

When you bring up the topic of the engagement ring, if he says something like, "Don't worry about it," or "I've got it covered," there's no need to freak out, because:

1. The odds are good that he knows your taste.

2. If he felt he didn't know your taste, he was probably smart enough to ask your sister and/or best friend for help.

3. When it's time to get the wedding band, you can go to every jewelry store in North America and try on rings to your heart's content.

The truth, however, is that these days most guys are glad to talk about the wedding ring with you. Since it's one of the most expensive things he'll ever buy, he wants to be sure he's getting you what you want! He'll be glad to have you point him in the right direction.

There are a couple of different ways you can do this:

♥ Tell him if you have a family ring. If Grandma Rose left you a diamond in her will, your boyfriend needs to know that before he goes out and spends his life savings on something you already have.

♥ Show him pictures in a magazine. Don't be afraid to tear the pictures out and hand them to him—that way, he can show the salesman in the jewelry store.

♥ Point out a friend's ring that you really like. Just be sure he knows NOT to get you an exact replica. That's awkward.

♥ Pointing out designs in a jewelry store window. If he wants some element of surprise by not actually going into a store together, you can still window shop. Every mall and Main Street in America has a jewelry store. Even if the place you're walking by isn't where he wants to buy the ring, they're still going to have a window display that can help give you both ideas.

♥ Go shopping together before the engagement. What's nice about doing it this way is that you know you'll get something you want (and you know it will be the right size). Plus, there's still an element of surprise because you won't see the final product until the big night.

♥ Go shopping together after you're engaged. This method is for the woman who wants total control over the ring design and leaves nothing to chance. I'm not a fan of this method because there's no element of surprise. Plus, once you tell people you're engaged, they're going to want to see the ring—and you're going to want to show it to them—but it may not be ready for several months.

Step #4: Wait

This is the hardest step of them all. You've had the marriage conversation. You've gone and looked at ring styles, and now there's nothing to do but wait. Your boyfriend wants the night you get engaged to be the greatest night of your life. And he also wants there to be an element of surprise, even if you went ring shopping together. So don't offer to help him plan the engagement. And please don't ask him when it's happening, because that just spoils everything. Go about your life as normally as you can. The big moment will be coming soon.

Here's the thing, Janis. I've been going about my business normally now for a few weeks, and he still hasn't popped the question. We went ring shopping together, so I know it's coming. Can't I say something eventually?

You don't have to wait forever. But you should wait a lot longer than you think before asking him when he's going to pop the question. I'd recommend waiting *at least* three months after you go shopping before bringing up the subject.

Three months?!

Yes, three months! I know it seems like an eternity, but it's really not. Planning an engagement takes a lot longer than you realize. Here's why:

♥ Time. If he's having a special setting made for the ring, it can sometimes take well over a month to get it done. And he can't pop the question without the ring!

♥ Logistics. If he's planning something very elaborate for the engagement night, it can take a while to arrange all the details. I know that it doesn't take three months to make a dinner reservation. But the beautiful hotel down on the beach where he wants to pop the question may be booked up for the next few weeks.

♥ Availability. Even though you're both eager to get engaged, your boyfriend will want to pop the question on a weekend when you're both free. Business travel, a houseguest, or someone else's wedding can all get in the way.

♥ Upcoming family event. If there's a big family event on the horizon—Thanksgiving, Grandma's Jane's eighty-fifth birthday, a family reunion at the Grand Canyon—many guys will want to wait until just before the gathering to pop the question. That way, you can have a large celebration with everyone soon afterward.

♥ The element of surprise. As I've said, guys love catching you a little off guard when they propose. So, if you've just gone ring shopping, he may want to wait a few extra weeks just to keep it a surprise.

I doubt you'll ever get to three months between ring shopping and marriage proposal . . . and that's part of the reason I suggested that time frame. When women freak out most of the time it's been only about two weeks. Relax. He knows what he's doing. You've waited many, many years for this to happen—what's another week or two?

Besides, once he has the ring, he isn't going to wait long. The ring will be burning a hole in his pocket—he'd rather see it on your finger than in his closet.

Now, if it really has been an eternity and you're curious about what he's planning, you can always ask him about the engagement without really asking him.

How do you do that?

Easy—just show him another picture from a magazine of a ring you like and ask him what he thinks. If he says something like, "Well . . . it's nice, but maybe you can get that ring on our twenty-fifth anniversary," then you know he already has a ring and is planning to give it to you soon.

If that still doesn't work, then you can go the direct route and say something like, "Sweetie, I love you, but it's been six months since we went ring shopping. So, what's the deal?"

Not What You're After

This is probably the easiest (and most obvious) "Not What You're After" section in the whole book. Earlier I talked about the different reactions your boyfriend can have when you bring up the "status of the relationship" conversation. But the worst response is when he just blows you off.

He says something like: "Marriage?! I don't want to talk about this," and then he walks out of the room.

That reaction is MUCH worse than him saying he doesn't want to get married, because at least your boyfriend is being honest if he says he doesn't think you're soul mates. But when your boyfriend doesn't say anything at all, he's being a jackass. He's taking something that's obviously important to you and treating it like dirt.

Clearly, he doesn't want to marry you. But he doesn't want to break up with you either because he likes the companionship and the sex. Unacceptable!

A guy who wants to be your husband will be happy to talk about marriage. Even those guys who still haven't made up their minds understand that it's normal to at least talk about the subject.

> "At eighteen months, if I haven't asked her to marry me, I break up with her. It isn't going anywhere and we probably both know that by then."
>
> —Roger, Baltimore, MD

Obviously, that quote doesn't apply to everyone. Many couples need more than a year and a half to decide if they want to get married. And some couples may know a lot sooner than that.

But the point is that by a year and a half, you'll both know whether you're heading toward marriage or not. Trust me— by that point in the relationship, he's already made up his mind, even if he's too much of a coward to say what he's thinking.

Let Him Down Easy

Any doubts you have about marrying your boyfriend should be discussed *before* he goes ring shopping. It's very hard to say no when he's down on one knee and offering you a diamond ring worth thousands of dollars. And I'll tell you one thing: No man EVER wants his marriage proposal rejected. But saying yes if you don't mean it is even worse.

So don't put yourself in that lose-lose situation. If you're not sure he's the one for you, this is your last chance. Talk to him NOW. Otherwise, you may screw up his emotions for a long, long time.

CHAPTER 15

He Hopes He Knows
Your Answer

Getting Engaged

By now, you both know how to make each other happy. I mean, he wouldn't be proposing if the two of you weren't completely compatible. So, at this point, you probably don't need any more advice from me . . . but I can't resist! (Are you really surprised?)

Here are a few final tips to make sure that one of the greatest nights of your life (and his life) lives up to expectations.

The Danger of Guessing

The first thing you should do to make the engagement go smoothly is to not announce to your friends that you're absolutely positive tonight is the night. I'm sure that at some point you've been part of a conversation that goes like this:

Woman: I think tonight is the big night.

Friend: Really?

Woman: Yep. Michael's made reservations at my favorite bistro. It's very romantic. And he told me that it was very important—no rescheduling dinner to go to the movies with friends.

Friend: This is so exciting!
Woman: I know! I'm trying to stay calm!

Once you've made the prediction that you're getting engaged tonight, it's pretty much the kiss of death. Inevitably, you don't wind up getting engaged that night, which leaves you totally bummed out. And then, to add insult to injury, you have to tell your friends that you were wrong:

Friend: Let me see the ring.
Woman: Um . . . we didn't get engaged.
Friend: What happened?
Woman: Nothing. It was just dinner.
Friend: Why was it so important to him that you not cancel?
Woman: Oh, the bistro was having a wine special. Buy a bottle, get a second one half price. Michael really wanted to go.

Your boyfriend isn't intentionally trying to fake you out—but sometimes it just happens accidentally. And if your friends are expecting to see a ring the next day, it makes your boyfriend look like a jerk . . . even if he's not. So you can guess in your mind whether tonight is THE NIGHT, but don't share those thoughts with anyone else.

An Official Answer

When he does finally pop the question, your mind will be racing too fast to remember much of anything. But, hopefully, deep in the corner of your brain, you'll remember the following:

♥ Try your best to listen to whatever speech he's giving. After clients of mine get engaged, they always tell me that they prepared a very romantic speech, but the woman wasn't listening. All she was doing was staring at the ring. The solution for him, of course, is not to take out the ring until after he's made the speech, but if he forgets, try to listen to what he's saying for as long as he can . . . even as the diamond calls to you. He's chosen his words for this moment carefully and he really wants you to hear them.

♥ If your answer is yes, say it. Aloud. It's a funny thing, but when a guy asks for your hand in marriage, he wants to hear the actual word *yes* escape from your lips. For him, that's the moment when he can celebrate. The longer you sit there speechless, the quicker he'll go into a panic. So say yes, aloud, and then you can start to hyperventilate with joy.

♥ Spend a little time together before you call everyone on the planet. There are tons of friends and family who need to know the news. But an engagement is a very personal event between the two of you. So don't forget to celebrate alone for a bit before picking up the phone and calling everyone you know.

♥ Don't be annoyed if you find out that he's asked your dad for permission. A lot of women tell me they're upset to learn that their boyfriend called her dad to ask permission. To many women, it seems like an outdated custom. And it's even a little chauvinistic: A woman isn't "property" like she was hundreds of years ago. Plus, it ruins the surprise when you call your parents because they already know that you got engaged.

But here's the thing: Asking parental permission for your hand in marriage doesn't mean your boyfriend and father are planning your life without you. In fact, it's not even asking permission—your dad knows that if he says no, you'll probably get married anyway.

So why make the call?

The answer, quite simply, is that it's a sign of respect toward your dad. Your boyfriend is joining your family, and fathers LOVE the formality of welcoming a new son on board. Trust me, your dad will be thrilled your boyfriend called. With that one phone call, your new fiancé has done more to endear himself to your dad than twenty years of playing golf (and letting your dad win) ever could. Plus, if you're lucky, your dad has kept his mouth shut and you can still surprise your mom with the fabulous news.

The adrenaline will pretty much take over at this point. Lots of women—including myself—don't even remember all the details of getting engaged because they're going through such a rush of emotions. But your reflexes will serve you well. It's okay for your brain not to function because it's overloaded with happiness.

What an Interesting Setting You Chose!

After the initial shock of getting engaged has worn off (sometimes this takes an hour, sometimes it takes ten years), you may have the one negative thought enter your head:

I'm madly in love and I'm beyond thrilled to be engaged. But the ring isn't my style at all. Am I now a horrible person for thinking that? And what should I do? Wear a ring I hate?

You are not a horrible person for thinking those thoughts, but it is horrible if you say any of that aloud. Seriously. Throughout this book, I've stressed the importance of loving your boyfriend more than his wealth. If you make a negative comment about the ring, you're going to send him the wrong message. He's going to think you're more interested in the ring than him. Or he's going to think that he's blown it and maybe he really can't make you happy after all.

Now, here's when some women interrupt me and say:

No, no, Janis. You misunderstand. It's isn't the size of the diamond or the cost of the ring that I'm complaining about. It's the cut of the stone and the style of the setting.

I understand the difference, but your boyfriend won't . . . at least not on the night you get engaged.

But Janis, shouldn't he know my sense of style? We're getting married! Are we making a big mistake?

Only you will know for certain if you're making a mistake, but the fact that you don't like the ring setting doesn't mean you should call off the whole thing. Even if he did his homework, he may have picked out a ring that's different from one that you would have chosen. But that's okay.

Down the road, you can say things like, "I feel like I don't need any more jewelry with yellow gold. I'm sort of in love with platinum." (Although, for the record, there are worse things in life than a husband who buys you too much yellow gold!)

But for the night you get engaged, here's my advice: Worship whatever ring he's picked out for you because it's a sign of his love. As beautiful as the ring is, it represents something infinitely more special. If it doesn't fit, or there's something else wrong, you can deal with it later. Tonight, the ring is perfect because he gave it to you.

The Best News of All

And now the most important news in this whole chapter (and, frankly, the whole book): What men want once you're engaged is exactly what you want.

When he slides the engagement ring onto your finger, something magical happens. Actually, a lot of magical things happen! But one of the best is that what he's looking for and what you're looking for are now one and the same.

Oh, sure, you may have some disagreements down the road about how many people to invite to the wedding or where you should spend Thanksgiving, but that's not what I'm talking about. I'm talking about the *big* stuff. The stuff that *really* matters. That's where the two of you are now on the same page . . . and will be forever. Because what he wants when you get engaged is:

♥   To love you.
♥   To take care of you.
♥   To always be honest with you.
♥   To be with you forever.

Pretty great, huh?!

Not What You're After

No more warnings from me, ladies. Your new fiancé is the man you've always been after. You've found him. You're engaged. You've done it. It's wonderful. Congratulations!

Let Him Down Easy

Hopefully, there won't be any need to "Let Him Down Easy" after the engagement, because once the ring is on the finger, there's no "easy" way to call things off. So let me recommend this: Sometime before the wedding, have a sit-down with your ceremony officiant. As you discuss what you want the officiant to say during the ceremony, let him or her ask you guys a few hard-hitting questions about your relationship. This will allow the officiant to get to know the two of you better—and you'll get to know each other even better as well.

Having a mini couples–therapy session before the wedding is nothing to be embarrassed about. Lots of people do it. In fact, lots of religious officiants require it before they marry you. That way, you can both work out any jitters you have about getting married.

Conclusion

Ladies, you're now ready to go find the guy of your dreams! But before you do, there's one more thing you have to know. It's the most important lesson in the whole book, and that's why I've saved it for last:

> THE RIGHT GUY WILL BE SOMEONE WHO SPENDS AS MUCH TIME THINKING ABOUT WHAT YOU WANT AS YOU DO ANALYZING WHAT HE WANTS.

You have just invested the time it takes to read this book and learn about what men want. Naturally, I'm thrilled and think that shows just how serious you are about trying to find the right guy.

Buy you must—MUST—hold men to the same standard. They don't have to read a book on the subject (I haven't written one for them yet!), but they should be doing whatever they can to learn about you and make you happy. It's as simple as that.

In this book, I've discussed how it's nice to plan a diversion if your boyfriend is having a bad week or to buy him a bottle of his favorite Scotch on his birthday. But he must return the sentiment. Your boyfriend should want to wear a certain jacket because you think it looks awesome. He should want to bring you to a Willie Nelson concert on Valentine's Day because he knows you love country music.

When a guy cares about you, he does these thoughtful things instinctively and effortlessly. Don't you dare settle for any excuses! How many women do you know who say things like "Gary's a really great guy when we're alone," or "You just don't know him like I do." You deserve better.

It's time to wake up and face reality. Dating should always be a two-way street. If you get your boyfriend a designer watch for his birthday and he gets you some tennis balls, there's a problem.

Remember: Crappy boyfriends usually act the way they do because they think you can't get anyone better. They're preying on your insecurities. But there's no need to be insecure any more. You can find the right guy. You've made it through this book, so you know what decent men are looking for. All that's left for you to do is take what you've learned and use it to make your dating life better and more successful.

I wish you luck . . . but you won't need it!

Resource Guide

So you've read the book and now your head is spinning with new ideas for how to invigorate your dating life. Only there's one problem:

Okay, Janis, I get that guys like it if I get my hair blown out before a first date. But where exactly should I go?

Never fear, Janis is here! Now, before I give you some of my own recommendations, remember that it's not about how much you spend, it's about how you *feel*. I want you to be sexy and confident, but you don't have to be wearing Armani in order to accomplish that. Many of you live in places that may not be fashion capitals of the world. And even if you're in New York or L.A., you may not feel like spending the money to have Vidal Sassoon himself give you a blow out. That's totally fine. Remember: the guy isn't going to see the label on your clothes; he's going to see *you*. (And even if the clothes come off, let's hope he's still more interested in you than the clothes!)

That said, I get asked for recommendations all the time, and, of course, I'm happy to give them. Most of these places are in New York City, because that's where I live. In order for me to recommend a place, I must check it out personally and send at least two girls from my office on follow-up visits. Bottom line: if it's here, it's good.

My website, www.janisspindelmatchmaker.com, also has a "Janis's Best Of" section that's continually updated, so you can visit the site at any time for more ideas.

Acupuncture

Eastside Healing Arts
James M. Strickler, L.Ac., Dipl.Ac.
201 East 67th Street, 5th Floor
New York, NY 10021
212-772-2838

Bodywork

Helene Kaye—Essential Bodywork
New York, NY
212-744-7240

Ballroom Dance Lessons

Empire Dance
127 West 25th Street, 11th Floor
New York, NY 10001
212-645-2441
www.empiredance.com

Stepping Out Studios
37 West 26th Street, 9th Floor
New York, NY 10010-1006
646-742-9400
646-742-0681 (fax)
www.steppingoutstudios.com

Chiropractor

Dr. Stephen Weinberg
50 Lexington Avenue, Suite LL3
New York, NY 10001
212-995-1515
212-995-2335 (fax)

Cosmetic Dentistry

Jennifer Jablow, DDS
120 East 56th Street, 6th floor
New York, NY 10021
212-752-5929
www.doctorjablow.com

NYC Smile Design
Dr. Elisa Mello and Dr. Ramin Tabib
8 East 84th Street
New York, NY, 10028
212-452-3344
212-412-9005 (fax)
www.nycsmiledesign.com

Cosmetic Orthodontics

Dr. Josh Z. Epstein
800 Tennent Road
Manalapan, NJ 07726
732-536-4422
732-536-3396 (fax)
www.braceplace.com

Dr. Jessica Greenberg and Dr. Jennifer Salzer
111 Broadway, Suite 1707
New York, NY 10006
212-871-9835
www.invisalignwallstreet.com

Dating Coach

Janice D. Bennett, Ph.D.
New York, NY
212-874-1470
212-787-3369 (fax)
www.doctorlovecoach.com

Day Spas

Acqua Beauty Bar
7 East 14th Street
New York, NY 10003
212-620-4329
212-627-5129 (fax)
www.acquabeautybar.com

Sphatika International
1841 Broadway, Suite 811
New York, NY 10022
212-265-5885
www.sphatika.com

The Style Bar
1 Bay Street
Sag Harbor, NY 11963

631-725-6730
631-725-6733 (fax)
www.stylebarspa.com

Dermatology

Sadick Aesthetic Surgery & Dermatology
911 Park Avenue
New York, NY 10021
212-772-7242

and

833 Northern Boulevard, Suite 130
Great Neck, NY 11021
516-482-8040
www.sadickdermatology.com

Dr. Howard Sobel, MD, F.A.A.C.S.Y
Skin & Spa Cosmetic Surgery Center
960A Park Avenue
New York, NY 10028
212-288-0060
212-879-4598 (fax)
www.drsobel.com

Electrolysis

Barbara Leibowitz, C.P.E.
Herald Towers
50 West 34th Street
New York, NY 10001
212-239-0783
www.electrolysisnyc.com

Esthetician

Michele Sabino, Clinical Esthetician
1009 Fifth Avenue
New York, New York 10028
212-472-1800
www.drimber.com

Eyewear

Alain Mikli
Boutique New York 57
575 Madison Avenue
New York, NY 10022
212-751-6085

and

Boutique New York 76
986 Madison Avenue
New York, NY 10021
212-472-6085
212-472-1974 (fax)
www.mikli.com

Felice Dee Eyewear
69 East 71st Street
New York, NY 10021
212-717-7062

Florist

Mille Fiori Floral Design
227 West 29th Street, 2nd Floor
New York, NY 10001

212-714-2202, extension 11
212-714-2130 (fax)
www.millefioriflowers.com

Hair Salons

Christo Fifth Avenue
574 Fifth Avenue, 5th Floor
New York, NY 10036
212-997-8800
www.curlisto.com

Roy Teeluck Salon
38 East 57th Street
New York, NY 10022
212-888-2221
www.royteelucksalon.com

ValeryJoseph
1044 Madison Ave
New York, NY 10022
212-517-7377

and

820 Madison Avenue
New York, NY 10021
212-517-2333
www.valeryjoseph.com

The Salon and Day Spa @ Amagansett Square
P.O. Box 2729
Amagansett, NY 11930
631-267-6677
631-267-0773 (fax)

Image Consultant

Elena Castenada
351 East 84th Street, Suite 11A
New York, NY 10028
212-879-5790
www.newyorkimageconsultant.com

Laser Hair Removal

Romeo & Juliette Laser Hair Removal Center
38 East 57th Street, 3rd Floor
New York, New York 10022
212-750-2000
www.romeojuliettelaserhairremoval.com

Lingerie

Bra Tenders
630 Ninth Avenue, Suite 601
New York, NY 10036
212.957.7000 or 888-GET-A-BRA

Makeup Artists

Laura Geller
1044 Lexington Avenue
New York, NY 10021
212.570.5477 or 800-MAKE UP-4
212-570-5521 (fax)
www.laurageller.com

Vincent Longo
49 West 37th Street, 12th Floor
New York, NY 10018
212-777-2367 or 1-877-LONGO-99
212-472-1614 (fax)
www.vincentlongo.com

Beautiful Faces Makeup & Hair Studio
Gail Sagel, Creator
139 Post Road East
Westport, CT 06880
203-226-1818
www.facesbeautiful.com

Nutritionists

Joy Bauer
116 East 63rd Street
New York, NY 10021
212-759-6999, extension 1
www.joybauernutrition.com

Carmen Fusco, M.S., C.D.N., C.N.S.
333 East 43rd Street, Suite 114
New York, NY 10017
212-983-6383
www.rejuvenex.net

Oz Garcia, PhD/Personal Best
10 West 74th Street, Suite 1G
New York, NY 10023
212-362-5569
www.ozgarcia.com

Personal Trainers

Spindel Sports Academy
Allen Spindel
New York, NY
917-882-5200
www.spindelsportsacademy.com

Yes, Allen is my husband! But that's not his only qualification. He earned a bachelor's degree in physical education from Oklahoma City University and a master's degree in physical education from Emporia State University. He's also a nationally certified personal trainer and group fitness trainer and is a member of the National Strength and Conditioning Association.

Pilates

Power Pilates
multiple locations in New York City, Chicago, and
southern California
212-627-5852
www.powerpilates.com

Stationery

Invite & Write (by appointment only)
Bunny Shestack
330 7th Avenue, 18th Floor
New York, NY 10001
212-594-5942

Therapists

Daniel Aferiat, CSW
Life Management Consultants
330 West 58th Street, Suite 410
New York, NY 10019
212-974-9722

Rachel A. Sussman, CSW
Licensed Clinical Social Worker and Marriage and
Family Therapist
85 Fifth Avenue, Suite 934
New York, NY 10003
212-769-0533
www.sussmancounseling.com

Unique Dates

Little Shop of Crafts
431 East 73rd Street
New York NY 10021
212-717-6636
212-717-0631 (fax)
www.littleshopny.com

Yoga

Yoga Works
multiple locations in New York and California
212-647-9642 (YOGA)
www.yogaworks.com